Approaching the Nuclear Tipping Point

Approaching the Nuclear Tipping Point

Cooperative Security in an Era of Global Change

James E. Goodby

ROWMAN & LITTLEFIELD
Lanham • Boulder • New York • London

Published by Rowman & Littlefield
A wholly owned subsidiary of The Rowman & Littlefield Publishing Group, Inc.
4501 Forbes Boulevard, Suite 200, Lanham, Maryland 20706
www.rowman.com

Unit A, Whitacre Mews, 26–34 Stannary Street, London SE11 4AB

British Library Cataloguing in Publication Information Available

Library of Congress Cataloging-in-Publication Data

978-1-4422-6570-7 (cloth)
978-1-4422-6571-4 (paper)
978-1-4422-6572-1 (electronic)

In Memoriam
Sidney Drell
1926–2016

CONTENTS

PREFACE

The conceptual underpinnings of this book came to me from one of the nation's greatest Secretaries of State, George P. Shultz, with whom I worked at the Department of State in the 1980s and again at Stanford University's Hoover Institution from 2007 to the present. "The world is awash in change," he is fond of saying, and he draws conclusions from that observation that have profound implications for the United States and its role in the world. George Shultz speaks of "a global commons," and he is not using the classical definition when he says that. He means there are threats to humanity's existence that require a common response because no nation acting alone can prevent a catastrophe. To him, this challenge to governance is a top priority for serious thinkers everywhere. As an economist, he appreciates how important the institutions created by farsighted people after the Second World War have been in helping to prevent the economic disasters that occurred after the First World War and paved the way for the Second. As a statesman, he sees that new institutions are needed to manage the existential challenges of our times—climate change and its effects and the ever-present prospect of a nuclear holocaust. As a citizen, he has spoken out repeatedly for policies that will make America and the world safer.

George Shultz has a keen interest in science and its immense capacity for both good and evil in human affairs. This led to his remarkably productive collaboration with two other colleagues at Stanford, former Secretary of Defense William Perry and the noted nuclear physicist Dr. Sidney Drell.

Just as I came to Hoover ten years ago, these three men began a campaign, later joined by Henry Kissinger and Sam Nunn, to rekindle the spirit that led President Reagan and Soviet General Secretary Gorbachev to consider eliminating nuclear weapons during their historic meeting in 1986 at Reykjavik, Iceland.

While William Perry was Under Secretary, Deputy Secretary, and finally Secretary of Defense, he introduced several technological innovations into U.S. defense programs that made possible a new strategy that is less reliant on nuclear weapons and that are still in the forefront of American military capabilities today. Sharing George Shultz's vision of a world without nuclear weapons, Perry has worked tirelessly in recent years to remind younger generations of the threat that nuclear weapons present to the survival of our civilization and what can and must be done to save humanity from a descent into another Dark Age. He has been an inspiration to me as I have thought about how I could speak to successor generations about the nuclear legacy they are inheriting.

My dear friend and colleague, Sid Drell, with whom I had an exceptionally fruitful professional relationship for three decades, passed away on December 21, 2016. He was one of the wisest men I have ever known, his counsel always realistic and farsighted. This book draws heavily on the work that he and I did together over the years on our shared causes—a nuclear test ban and preventing nuclear proliferation.

I have been very fortunate in these last years to live in the heart of Silicon Valley. The impact of technology on society has never been greater than it is at the present time and much of that technology and its applications emanated from right here. A lot of my exploration of that theme in this book is speculative because the revolution is still under way. I have no one to blame but myself for what I say about that.

It was fortuitous that I began to write this book just as the 2016 U.S. presidential election got started. This was clearly a "change election," and the political, social, and economic issues that were debated in this period necessarily inform much of what I have written. My only regret is that the writing of this book must come to an end just as America's experiment with democratic governance is entering a new phase.

I began working on nuclear issues in 1954 at the U.S. Atomic Energy Commission and was assigned almost immediately to be an assistant on disarmament matters to Dr. John von Neumann, an AEC commissioner and one of the great minds of that or any other era. My last assignment in the U.S. government was in year 2000 as deputy to General John Shalikashvili, former Chairman of the Joint Chiefs of Staff, who had been asked by President Clinton to explore with senators what could be done to advance the prospects for their consent to ratification of the Comprehensive Test Ban Treaty. It says a lot for our country that two men born in Eastern Europe could contribute so much to their adopted nation and to the world. I was privileged to work with them and with many other great Americans and friends from other nations during my long career in public service.

I have tried to be as objective as I could be in writing this book but convictions derived from a lifetime of working for peace and security among nations have guided me as I sought to understand where we as a nation have come from in the nuclear age and where we might want to go in the future.

—James E. Goodby
Hoover Institution, Stanford University
Stanford, California
June 2017

ACKNOWLEDGMENTS

The Flora Family Foundation provided essential financial support for this project as part of grants to the Hoover Institution. I am grateful to the foundation and to Esther and Walter Hewlett for this and for their continuing confidence in our work at Hoover.

Several friends of long standing who are experts and scholars of the issues discussed in this book provided insights and recommendations which resulted in serious improvements in the text. They include Dr. James Timbie, Dr. Raymond Jeanloz, and Dr. Edward Ifft.

My son, Dr. Laurence Goodby, and my daughter-in-law, Lucy Geever, provided advice and reality checks throughout the research and writing. My wife, Priscilla, as always, gave me so much support that I think of her as my coauthor.

Summer Takash and Zachary Schwermann helped with the early drafts of the manuscript. Three friends at the Hoover Institution were key to the production of this book. They are: Susanni Ngarian, Rebecca Berman, and Susan Schendel. They helped me with research, offered advice and comments on the manuscript, gave me much-needed editorial assistance, and transcribed all of my handwriting to what the reader sees today. They are real professionals and I am deeply grateful to them.

Marie-Claire Antoine, former senior acquisition editor at Rowman & Littlefield, and her successor Mary Malley, championed my ideas for a book and gave me encouragement as I wrote it. Thanks to them, and Elaine McGarraugh, senior production editor, a book emerged. An author could not ask for more.

James E. Goodby

Introduction

The title of this book sums up its central argument: we are fast approaching a time when nuclear weapons might escape the restraints that American diplomacy has sought to impose on them. The outlook for success in reducing nuclear weapons or even preventing an increase in their numbers, especially in unstable regions of the world, has become clouded in the last few years. It would be a major miracle if many more years were to go by without nuclear weapons being used in a war for the first time since 1945.

A nuclear war is not a long-term, over-the-horizon, abstract issue. It is an ever-present possibility with many potential triggers. Even a "small" nuclear war, which could break out on short or no notice, has the capacity to inflict major damage on the global environment and kill hundreds of thousands, perhaps millions, of people. Only close and sustained cooperation among many nations can prevent a catastrophe, but changes affecting the international system in the last few years have cast doubt on the future of cooperative security.

In large parts of the world, citizens have been empowered to an unprecedented degree by the ability to rapidly acquire and disseminate information through the Internet and social media. One might think that a better understanding of people on the other side of the globe might make cooperation with their governments easier to achieve. Unprecedented empowerment has not yielded the advances in cooperative security that are essential to dealing with existential threats and to managing the "global commons." In fact, fragmentation and inward-looking populist movements have been the most striking effect.

In today's political and social environment, any discussion of the outlook for cooperative security has to be squarely embedded in the context of the ongoing backlash to global integration and the massive changes in the way human societies operate, thanks to technology. The widespread use of artificial intelligence and robotics, just to name two imminent game-changers, will certainly match and probably exceed the disruptions brought about by global economic integration, which, also thanks to technology, may already be reaching its peak.

Nationalism is on the rise in Western democracies, including the United

States, partly because citizens perceive globalization as the cause of lost jobs and a loss of their identity and place in society. This is partly because demographic changes, owing to migration from poor to rich nations and increased longevity, contribute to the sense of disruption in Europe and America. The sense of shock and resentment will accelerate when climate change drives people away from their homes in the equatorial zone toward northern climes.

Simultaneously with these disruptions, a power struggle has been under way to define, probably for centuries to come, the successor to the international system established in 1648 by the Peace of Westphalia that ended the Thirty Years' War. That settlement placed nation-states at the center of international relations and ended the debate about power distribution between supranational authorities such as the church and the states. In recent decades, global economic integration and the rise of powerful, privately owned economic organizations have created the conditions that have reopened debates about the distribution of power and authority in the international system.

Insufficiently recognized is still another factor that presents a serious challenge to Western representative democracies. Technology—and social media, in particular—is encouraging a form of direct democracy in which established institutions of governance are bypassed. Technological change has been a positive development in making life better for millions and millions of people around the globe. But it also has made governance through representative democracy more difficult to sustain. Social media have had a powerful effect on shaping public opinion and creating a form of "pure democracy," which *Federalist Paper No. 10*, written by James Madison, warned would encourage national fragmentation.[1]

If representative democracy is to remain the foundation of American governance in the future, the leaders the people choose to represent them will need to involve the people in decision making at an earlier stage than is often the case and will have to do a better job of informing them of the issues. This is a fundamental imperative for the future of representative democracy.

This book argues that a sour political atmosphere should not prevent a serious effort to address the threats we face. "In the long run we are all dead," said the economist John Maynard Keynes, and that truth has a poignant meaning when applied to questions about nuclear war.

As the world's most powerful nation, the United States could exercise decisive leadership in pointing the way to a safer future for all. A success in international cooperation to reduce and eliminate the nuclear threat to humanity would bolster international efforts to confront and control other existential challenges. Throughout its history, the United States has risen to meet challenges. That nuclear weapons have never been used in war since 1945 is largely the result of American-led statecraft. "The indispensable nation" is a title that was well earned. Leadership from America, backed by the American people, is needed once again. As President Trump said in his first speech to Congress, "The time for trivial fights is behind us."[2] How right that is!

NOTES

1. James Madison, "The Same Subject Continued: The Union as a Safeguard Against Domestic Faction and Insurrection," *The New York Packet*, November 23, 1787, https://www.congress.gov/resources/display/content/The + Federalist + Papers#TheFederalistPapers-10.

2. "Remarks by President Trump in Joint Address to Congress," https://www.whitehouse.gov/the-press-office/2017/02/28/remarks-president-trump-joint-address-congress.

ONE

Learning Survival Skills in the New World

The release of atom power has changed everything except our way of thinking.

—Albert Einstein

For generations now, humanity has been living, figuratively speaking, on the slopes of an active volcano, one that could erupt at any moment with little warning. If it did, the results would be felt worldwide. Even a limited nuclear war would have long-lasting effects on the climate and on agriculture. Images of Pompeii multiplied manyfold are apt. The cities of Hiroshima and Nagasaki and large numbers of their citizens were destroyed by blasts, firestorms, and radiation caused by two relatively small atomic bombs. Today, bombs and warheads far more powerful are plentiful.

Somehow, this condition has been normalized in people's minds. Hardly anybody thinks about it, although a nuclear war is the most serious short-term existential threat humanity faces. Existential threats such as this can only be met through global, regional, and bilateral cooperation among nations. No single nation, even the most powerful, acting on its own can remove existential threats. In a very real sense, the possessors of nuclear arsenals must act as stewards for all of humanity.

Nuclear war, of course, is not the only threat to the survival of human civilization and perhaps of the human race itself. Climate change is another, bringing with it a rise in sea levels, depriving some regions of their sources of water, and causing massive migration from equatorial zones to more habitable areas in the North. Pandemics are another potential existential threat. They can be caused by viruses resistant to treatment which are spread worldwide, aided by the hundreds of thousands of people who routinely travel from one country to another.

If only genuine and extensive cooperation among many nations can

5

stop a global catastrophe from happening, it is incumbent on governments, but also on every citizen, to examine how avoiding a nuclear catastrophe might be accomplished through global and regional cooperative actions among nations. To do this, we need to know how we got to this point. It began with a letter.

On August 2, 1939, Albert Einstein signed a letter to President Franklin D. Roosevelt warning him that recent scientific developments might make possible a powerful explosive based on nuclear fission and that scientists in Germany, then under Nazi rule, appeared to be acquiring uranium to investigate this possibility. The original letter had been drafted by the Hungarian physicist, Leo Szilard, then living in the United States and had been presented by him to Einstein in July at Einstein's summer home on Long Island.[1] Szilard reworked the letter after conversations with Einstein and returned with a new draft on August 2. Roosevelt received the letter several days after that and decided to establish a committee to advise him on a proper course of action and appointed Lyman Briggs, the director of the National Bureau of Standards, as its head.[2] The purpose was to investigate the potential of uranium as the basis for an atomic bomb. The Uranium Committee began its work in October 1939.[3] It quickly concluded that an atomic bomb might indeed be feasible and reported its findings to President Roosevelt.

The Manhattan Project was the eventual result of these initial studies. This was a vast and highly secret American project, run by the military in close collaboration with the scientific community, to build an atomic bomb. General Leslie Groves, the US Army Corps of Engineers officer who had recently overseen construction of the Pentagon, took command of the Manhattan Project.[4] Dr. J. Robert Oppenheimer, a leading American nuclear physicist, became the scientific director.[5] The British government had been working on a similar project, but lacking its own resources and being vulnerable to air attacks, it turned over all of its assets to the American project.

The advent of World War II persuaded America's top science administrators—people like Dr. Vannevar Bush of the Carnegie Institution of Washington, DC, and Dr. James Conant of Harvard—that mobilizing science for the war effort would require new and powerful government agencies to manage war-related scientific programs and to work closely with the military.

Facing the exigencies of World War II, the US government and the American scientific community rose to the occasion with an unprecedented display of organizational genius which could provide a model for a response to today's challenges. Vannevar Bush was the brain behind it. He persuaded Roosevelt to create the Office of Scientific Research and Development and became its director.[6] This office absorbed the Uranium

Committee and another new agency, the National Defense Research Committee, a subgroup of the National Academy of Sciences, headed by James Conant. American scientists and European scientists escaping from Nazi persecution joined as one in supporting the American war effort. One of them, Dr. Arthur Compton, a Nobel Prize–winning physicist and professor at the University of Chicago, worked closely with another Nobel Laureate, Enrico Fermi, an Italian physicist. They conducted early experiments on controlled nuclear fission in uranium and the possible use of plutonium, which is produced from uranium in nuclear reactors, as another route to an atomic bomb. Compton became head of the Metallurgical Laboratory of the Manhattan Project based at the University of Chicago.[7] Fermi, who held an appointment at Columbia University, moved to Chicago to help build a "pile," or nuclear reactor, with which they hoped to prove the concept of a controlled and sustained chain reaction in uranium, and thus the potential of this process both for energy and for production of plutonium.[8] This was successfully demonstrated by Enrico Fermi in an experiment conducted in a squash court under the stands of the University of Chicago's Stagg Field. The pile consisted of uranium oxide and graphite.[9]

News of the success was conveyed by telephone to James Conant, who was then at his Harvard office in Cambridge, Massachusetts, by Arthur Compton, who was with Fermi at the Met Lab in Chicago. The beginning of the nuclear age has several contenders for the most plausible date, but December 2, 1942, is one of the most convincing. On that date a sustained chain reaction was proved to be feasible.[10]

What Arthur Compton said in guarded language in his telephone call to Conant informing him of the result is memorable not only for what it announced but also for what it foretold. Referring to Enrico Fermi, who had fled Mussolini's Italy, Compton said, "The Italian navigator has just landed in the new world."[11] How right that message was. The world had changed forever on that day. Looking back from a perspective of nearly seven decades later, two former US Secretaries of State, George Shultz and Henry Kissinger, a former US Secretary of Defense, William Perry, and a former Chair of the US Senate Armed Services Committee, Sam Nunn, described the ultimate result of the experiment and its challenge in equally apt and allegorical terms: "Our age has stolen fire from the gods. Can we confine this awesome power to peaceful purposes before it consumes us?"[12]

From the very inception of the Manhattan Project, mounted by the Roosevelt administration in 1941, two months before Pearl Harbor, the scientists involved realized that the atom bomb was not just a bigger explosive device. They worried that it might have enormous destructive consequences they could not predict. Scientists from Britain and refugee scientists from continental Europe joined with American scientists in a shared belief that the new weapon would have to be subject to international control if humanity was to survive in the new world they had created.

Political leaders were slower to reach that conclusion. The administration of Harry Truman, who became US president when Roosevelt died in office on April 12, 1945, tested a nuclear device in July 1945 and then used the two atomic bombs it then had for the first and only time in human history in a war in August 1945.[13] In the circumstances that existed then, it would have been difficult for the president not to use the bomb, which had been developed at great cost during a period of daily carnage in the European and Pacific theaters and which was seen by those who knew about it as a game-changer in World War II. Roosevelt already had agreed with Churchill at a meeting on September 18, 1944, at his home in Hyde Park, New York, that it might be used against the Japanese.[14] Hitler, by the time of that agreement, was just months away from losing the war in Europe and from his death by suicide.

There had been discussions at high levels in Roosevelt's administration about international control, but no decisions had been made. Niels Bohr, a Dane and one of the world's foremost nuclear scientists, had urged Churchill and Roosevelt to inform the Soviet leader, Joseph Stalin, of the existence of the atomic bomb program before it became public knowledge. Bohr's advice was rejected. Churchill strongly believed that the atomic bomb should be a US-UK monopoly and persuaded Roosevelt, then in his last months of life, not to give Stalin any advance knowledge.[15] Churchill and Roosevelt saw the atomic bomb as a necessary asset for Britain if it was to play a strong role in a "United Nations," an idea then being studied as a method of creating world order in the postwar period. In fact, Stalin already knew about the project through spies in the United States.[16]

When Harry Truman took office, he knew nothing about the Manhattan Project. President Roosevelt had not shared that secret even with his own vice president. Truman quickly came to understand that international control of some sort would be necessary and appointed as heads of an advisory committee Dean Acheson, then the number two official at State, and David Lilienthal, head of the Tennessee Valley Authority, a large government-built, electricity-generating enterprise. Their work was guided and influenced by a team of scientists headed by Dr. J. Robert Oppenheimer, a firm believer in international control.[17]

Their Acheson-Lilienthal report became the basis for the Baruch Plan, named after Bernard Baruch, a Wall Street financier and advisor to presidents. Baruch introduced the plan at the United Nations on June 14, 1946. It called for the creation of an international authority to control the production of uranium and plutonium and ensure that they would be used only for peaceful purposes. Once the authority was up and running, the

United States would destroy any atomic bombs it then had. The US plan was countered by a Soviet demand that any US atomic bombs be destroyed first. The impasse lasted until the Soviet Union conducted its first test of an atomic bomb in 1949; thereafter, the Baruch Plan essentially became a dead letter.[18] The Soviet bomb test marked the beginning of a US-Soviet dialogue of the deaf that went nowhere until Joseph Stalin died in 1953 and was succeeded by a more flexible leadership. Thereafter, the US-Soviet dialogue became the centerpiece of international efforts to control and eliminate the nuclear threat, and that persisted throughout the Cold War. This channel is now in limbo because of differences between the two countries.

Since August 1945, when two American atomic bombs were detonated over Japan, Moscow and Washington have passed through six distinct phases in their efforts to control nuclear weapons, but also to turn them to their national advantage. This is summarized in table 1.

During phase one, which extended from 1945 to 1955, the stated goal of the United States was zero nuclear weapons and the establishment of an international authority to own and operate key nuclear operations to support nationally owned civilian nuclear power plants. Stalin, then in his last years as ruler of the Soviet Union, intended to have a Soviet nuclear arsenal and so insisted on US weapons being destroyed while Soviet scientists worked on their own atomic bomb. In Washington, many in Congress and elsewhere thought that the future security of the United States required a nuclear arsenal and ample production facilities. Thus, for the first ten years of the nuclear age, dead-end talks and posturing for public relations advantages dominated the Moscow-Washington relationship. The US–Soviet Cold War competition made this situation almost inevitable, but the Korean War plus McCarthyism at home and shoring up alliance arrangements abroad were priorities for the Truman administration and Eisenhower's first term. The technical challenges of developing thermonuclear weapons (hydrogen bombs) with a thousandfold or greater enhanced explosive yield than the fission weapons (atom bombs) that ended World War II also preoccupied US administrations.

From roughly 1955 to 1982, successive US presidents accepted that nuclear weapons were going to be part of the global scene for many years, and therefore determined that policies should be adopted that would make their use less likely. This involved basing nuclear weapons so as to discourage a first strike by an adversary, seeking stability in US–Soviet nuclear relations, and preventing the spread of nuclear weapons capabilities to other countries. This was a fruitful phase in terms of US-Soviet negotiations. It produced a Limited Test Ban Treaty, the Non-Proliferation Treaty, the Anti-Ballistic Missile Treaty, and the SALT I agreement.[19] Despite this, nuclear weapons arsenals in both the Soviet Union and the

Table 1. US-Soviet Cooperative Security (US Perspective)

US Presidents in Office	Six Phases	Concepts	Political Background	Results
Truman Eisenhower	"The Rules of the Game" 1945–1955	Eliminate nuclear weapons. Establish an international nuclear authority. General and complete disarmament.	Beginning of the Cold War Korean War McCarthyism Chinese Revolution	Spheres of interest in Europe
Eisenhower Kennedy Johnson Nixon Ford Carter	"Arms Control" Stability Discourage use 1955–1982	Make nuclear use less likely. Limit damage if war occurs. Prevent proliferation. Limit nuclear arms competition.	New Leaders in Moscow Thermonuclear weapons Vietnam War MRIVs/BMD Berlin	LTBT NPT ABM Treaty SALT I
Reagan Bush I	"Nuclear Abolition" 1982–1992	Eliminate nuclear weapons. Build strategic defenses.	Reagan Revolution Gorbachev Revolution	CBMs CFE Treaty INF Treaty PNIs START
Clinton	"Yugoslavia with Nukes" 1993–2001	Prevent loss or theft of nuclear weapons. Preserve ABM Treaty. Limit nuclear arms competition.	Polarization in US politics US economy enjoying good times Globalization	Nunn-Lugar Program
Bush II	"America Unbound" 2001–2008	Limit restraints on US ability to build nuclear forces, especially defenses.	Unipolar moment 9/11 Prevent war Nukes bad if held by "bad guys" Iraq, Afghanistan	SORT ABM abrogation PSI Res.1540
Obama	"Back to the Future" 2009–2017	Eliminate nuclear weapons through US-Russian agreements followed by agreements with other nations, including restraint measures.	Polarization Recession	New START Nuclear security summits

United States continued to grow, peaking in 1966–1967 in the United States and in 1986 in the Soviet Union.[20] Several near misses occurred in terms of nuclear accidents, and a nuclear war was narrowly averted during the Cuban Missile Crisis. A competition for global support by the two superpowers resulted in a division of the world into two hostile camps and a group of neutral and nonaligned nations.

The third phase began in 1982 with the efforts by Ronald Reagan and Mikhail Gorbachev to start the process of negotiated reductions and ultimately the elimination of nuclear weapons. President George H. W. Bush picked up the baton in 1989 and added his own ideas, including reciprocal unilateral measures to reduce the chances of a nuclear war that no one wanted. These were called "Presidential Nuclear Initiatives" (PNIs). This was a highly productive period in US-Soviet/Russian negotiations. It led to the Intermediate-Range Nuclear Forces Treaty to eliminate a whole class of US and Soviet nuclear weapons and produced the Strategic Arms Reduction Treaty (START) as well as parallel actions by the two governments to enhance cooperative security.[21] It was also President George H. W. Bush who recognized that the US arsenal fulfilled its core mission of deterrence, and therefore that the United States did not need new designs of nuclear weapons or weapons intended for new nuclear missions. Bush accepted a nuclear test moratorium, somewhat reluctantly, after Congress adopted a resolution requiring it.[22] The moratorium is still in effect.

The fourth phase focused on damage control after the collapse of the Soviet Union, a nuclear-armed superpower. The United States began to provide assistance to its former adversaries to enhance controls over fissile materials and expedite the nuclear reductions in Russia, Ukraine, Belarus, and Kazakhstan called for in the START agreement. Preventing the theft or loss of nuclear weapons and fissile materials was a high priority. This was the dominant theme from 1993 to 2001. It was not a time for important new nuclear reductions but it did succeed in preserving agreements from earlier years, such as the Anti-Ballistic Missile Treaty, and preventing loss of control of nuclear weapons.

The fifth phase spanned the two terms of President George W. Bush, from 2001 to 2009. It marked a turn away from US–Russian cooperative security efforts in the name of independent decision making by the United States, justified by the theory that arms control between Moscow and Washington was a relic of the Cold War. It did yield the US–Russia Strategic Offensive Reductions Treaty of 2002 and a series of multilateral antiterrorism agreements, such as the Proliferation Security Initiative (PSI) and UN Resolution 1540, aimed at preventing the spread of nuclear weapons.[23]

President Obama, in the sixth phase, returned to a policy that was consistent with Reagan's ideas about eliminating nuclear weapons. His administration negotiated a US-Russian agreement—New START—that extended and eventually superseded the Reagan-Bush START agreement, which expired in December 2009.[24] This sixth phase of the US–Soviet/ Russian nuclear relationship may continue into the future, but no negotiations to extend or expand it were under way as the Obama administration left office. It has laid the basis for future security cooperation between the two nations if they choose to seize the opportunity.

Bilateral negotiations between the United States and Russia to reduce nuclear weapons would be valuable, perhaps essential, given the preponderance of such weapons in their possessions. Other nations possessing nuclear weapons will need to be taken into account at some point. Various regional options are conceivable, as is a joint global enterprise undertaken by several nuclear-armed as well as non-nuclear-armed states. In a sense, that process already is under way with the UN General Assembly's adoption of Resolution L.41 in 2016 calling for a multilateral negotiation to outlaw the possession and use of nuclear weapons.[25]

LESSONS LEARNED

The pioneering security cooperation between Moscow and Washington during the first sixty-five years of the nuclear age cannot be a template for cooperation in this era of rapid global change. There are lessons in that history, however, that should be considered, even in the twenty-first century's very different environment. Some of these lessons could provide ideas about specific approaches that other nations could take to restrain nuclear arms. Other lessons are more abstract and certainly debatable, but important, nonetheless. Here are four of them:

- Cooperation between adversaries in developing rules of behavior is essential. Successful deterrence requires the acquiescence of both parties to the equation; it cannot be imposed by one party only.
- Avoiding unintended confrontations between adversaries must be a major task of statecraft; direct and sustained engagement between them is essential for this purpose.
- Radical reductions in the nuclear threat require changes in adversarial relationships; a cooperative political attack on the status quo is the only way to achieve this.
- Success in negotiating nuclear weapons constraints can contribute to an atmosphere in which cooperative security is a normal and expected part of international relationships.

To those familiar with the international order created by US-Soviet cooperation during the Cold War and the efforts during the last quarter of a century to build a consensus on an international order to replace it, these principles are familiar but still disputed. The history behind them is worth knowing and the lessons worth absorbing. In the following pages, I will recount, very briefly, some relevant history. An understanding of what happened and why can provide some of the answers to the question of how to build a peaceful and more stable international order in the twenty-first century, always considering that the Cold War is behind us and that states are going through a period of unusual chaos, largely because of the dizzying speed of change.

Adversarial Cooperation

The cockpit of the US-Soviet confrontation after World War II was Europe. The collapse of the American, British, and French attempts to reach a peace settlement with the Soviet Union left Germany divided and West Berlin separated from West Germany. At the end of the war, the division of occupation zones between Britain, France, and the United States, on the one hand, and the Soviet Union on the other, had left land access from the West to Berlin through East Germany. Access to Berlin could be cut off by Soviet forces based in East Germany. East Berlin eventually became the capital of East Germany—the German Democratic Republic. An Iron Curtain, as Winston Churchill put it in a speech in Fulton, Missouri, in 1946, had descended across Europe.[26] In the East, governments maintained power only with the permission and support of Moscow.

Despite rhetoric about changing that situation, the Western nations, including the United States, accepted it. Uprisings were suppressed by Soviet forces in East Berlin in 1953 and in Hungary in 1956, with no reaction from NATO, which, after all, had been founded in 1949 as a vehicle for collective defense of its members, not for rolling back the Iron Curtain by force. The strategy of containment, fully embraced by the Eisenhower administration after it took office in 1953, was a strategy of tolerating the status quo while waiting for changes to transform the Soviet Union from within. That did happen, but not until the 1980s. In the meantime, a tacit agreement, or modus vivendi, between Moscow and Washington, essentially supported by Washington's NATO allies, resulted in tolerating Soviet control over the Eastern European territory occupied in World War II. Finland and Norway in the north and Turkey in the south, the latter two members of NATO, were the only nations bordering on the Soviet Union in Europe that were not overrun by the Soviet army in World War II and escaped Soviet control after the war.

Whatever one may think about the necessity or the morality of such a bipolar sphere of interest system, it did regulate relations between two nuclear-armed superpowers for nearly forty years. When Soviet forces cut off land access to West Berlin in 1948, an airlift mounted mainly by the US Air Force kept the population of West Berlin stocked with necessary supplies. The actual use of nuclear weapons became a possibility only years later after Khrushchev threatened to hand over to East Germany control of access to the Western-occupied zone of West Berlin and to East Berlin.

Probably the omnipresent threat posed by nuclear weapons induced a sense of prudence, but the tacit agreement, or modus vivendi, on spheres of interest was at least as important in preventing the war that nobody wanted.

Successful Deterrence Also Requires Cooperation

When the Eisenhower administration took over from the Truman administration, Secretary of State John Foster Dulles announced a doctrine of "massive retaliation." The idea was that if Moscow tried to chip away at the American geopolitical situation through a series of small skirmishes that would weaken the United States without attacking it directly, the United States would respond with a massive retaliation, presumably nuclear, at a place and a time of its own choosing. Even before the end of the Eisenhower administration, that threat lost whatever credibility it might initially have had. The reason was that while no one, including Soviet leaders, doubted that the United States could devastate the Soviet Union many times over ("make the rubble bounce," as General Curtis LeMay put it), the development of a Soviet nuclear arsenal made it clear that the United States also would pay a heavy price. And so began mutual assured destruction (MAD). It induced prudence and helped avoid, generally, threatening autonomous moves. Its effect in underwriting the tacit spheres-of-influence policy in Europe was important.

Coercive atomic diplomacy to achieve lesser goals never worked because to make nuclear deterrence credible, the action which would justify the use of nuclear weapons by one party would have to be consequential enough to make the other party believe that nuclear war would be a likely result of taking that action. A Soviet invasion of NATO Europe was clearly and unequivocally defined by the United States as such an action. Leaders in both Moscow and Washington fairly quickly came to the conclusion that very few situations would justify a nuclear war, but one of them would be a Soviet attempt to take over Western Europe by force. Nuclear deterrence of such an attack came to be accepted in the Soviet Union and in the United States as one of the conditions that could enhance stable relations in Europe if properly managed by both sides.

How to do that was the subject of debate in nearly every US administration.

Avoiding Unintended Confrontations Requires Engagement
with Adversaries

Stability in relations between the Soviet Union and the United States was seriously threatened twice during the era when Nikita Khrushchev was general secretary and chairman of the Council of Ministers in Moscow. Both of the episodes were generated by Khrushchev's misperceptions about the ability of Soviet nuclear weapons to coerce the United States once the Soviet Union had acquired ballistic missiles that could target the United States and Western Europe. These episodes were exceptions to the modus vivendi between Moscow and Washington about avoiding autonomous actions that would test the limits of nuclear deterrence.

The first of these two dangerous episodes persisted over several years before a political settlement was reached. It concerned Khrushchev's determination to challenge the four-power status of Berlin. He evidently believed that Soviet breakthroughs in ballistic missile technology, as evidenced by the Sputnik success in 1957, gave Moscow new leverage that enabled it to coerce the West. Acting on this belief, Khrushchev initiated a series of crises over Western access to East Berlin and who controlled it. The crises were carefully controlled by both sides but the threat of using nuclear weapons came into play. Washington let it be known that it was considering the use of tactical nuclear weapons if military conflict arose over access. The crisis subsided and eventually a quadripartite agreement about Berlin was negotiated.

The second crisis—Cuba—was shorter, but much more intense. It began in secrecy in 1962 and rapidly became an uncontrolled confrontation in which the use of nuclear weapons was only narrowly averted. The story is well known and need not be retold here. It does need to be underscored that this was the most radical departure during the Cold War from the principle that nuclear deterrence could produce stability if it was jointly managed as an element of cooperative security. Khrushchev acted as an autonomous agent in this case rather than as a partner in the tightly controlled management of nuclear deterrence. It almost led to catastrophe.

Basic Change in the Practice of Deterrence Must Accompany and
Reinforce Basic Political Change in Relations Between Adversaries

The Truman administration was initially uncertain about the role that nuclear weapons should play in post–World War II defense plans. The US

Congress, decisively influenced by its Joint Committee on Atomic Energy, was never in doubt. Its leaders saw atomic bombs as the American "ace in the hole," wanted them to be an American monopoly, and wanted many of them. They were interested in what is today called nonproliferation but not in nonuse. They thought in terms of American superiority in nuclear weapons, not in terms of parity or reductions, and thought that the American monopoly would last for many years. In fact, it lasted only four years.

American strategic thinkers quickly realized that atomic bombs could not become normal weapons, as other technological innovations historically had become. Bernard Brodie was one of the first influential American strategists to express the thought that the purpose of nuclear weapons must be to prevent war. General, later President, Eisenhower shared that opinion, as did his military colleagues in Britain. As president, he decided to adopt a doctrine of reliance on nuclear deterrence, partly because he wanted to reduce the defense budget of the United States. He also favored negotiations with the Soviet Union to make war less likely. Almost from the beginning of his term in office in 1953, he reached out to Moscow and encouraged a dialogue with its leaders. After the death of Stalin in March 1953, that option became more feasible. Eisenhower proposed the International Atomic Energy Agency in 1953, launched a serious negotiation in London in 1957 on both conventional and nuclear constraints, and started a nuclear test moratorium and test ban negotiations in 1958. The Eisenhower test ban negotiations effectively ended with the Soviet downing of an American U-2 spy plane over Sverdlovsk, Ukraine, in May 1960, but he had laid the foundations for a successful outcome. Many of the norms and precedents of the nuclear age were established during Eisenhower's presidency, including the tradition of nonuse.

By the end of the Eisenhower administration, the United States and Britain had begun to discuss with the Soviet Union the idea of a moratorium on underground nuclear tests coupled with a treaty that would ban nuclear tests in the atmosphere, outer space, and under water. That is essentially the legal structure that exists today.

John F. Kennedy, taking office in January 1961, continued the negotiating effort and reached agreement with the Soviet Union on a Limited Test Ban Treaty in 1963.[27] None of these efforts by Truman, Eisenhower, or Kennedy headed off a nuclear arms race. In fact, nuclear doctrines in the United States broadly endorsed "arms control," which in its 1960 codification by Thomas Schelling and Morton Halperin was indifferent to numbers of nuclear weapons.[28] "Damage limitation," a targeting doctrine that sought to limit the number of warheads that could strike the United States or its allies, resulted in targeting Soviet nuclear bombers and missiles and so generated large numbers of aim points.

Not until President Ronald Reagan and Soviet general secretary, later president, Mikhail Gorbachev held office at the same time was it possible to attack the basic problems that divided the two countries. Arms control doctrine as a means of managing a buildup of nuclear arsenals gave way to the idea that nuclear weapons could be reduced and eliminated.

Reagan's policy was accompanied by major shifts in relations between East and West in Europe, as Gorbachev adopted a policy of ending the East-West confrontation in order to improve the Soviet economic situation. Gorbachev also introduced democratic structures in the Soviet Union and allowed this to happen in Eastern Europe. Because of these major policy changes, and because both Reagan and Gorbachev supported the elimination of nuclear weapons, it became possible to enter a period of sustained reductions in American and Russian nuclear forces. Budgetary constraints, of course, contributed to these reductions in the Soviet Union after 1986. This trend is now jeopardized by countervailing political developments in both nations.

President Gorbachev resigned as president of the Soviet Union on the evening of December 25, 1991, and the Soviet flag over the Kremlin was lowered for the last time after he spoke at midnight. This development—unforeseen except by George Kennan forty years earlier—followed a coup attempt by hardliners in Moscow that failed when Boris Yeltsin, then president of the Soviet Russian Republic, rallied the Russian people and the Soviet Army behind him. The leaders of Russia, Ukraine, and Belarus declared the formation of the Commonwealth of Independent States at a meeting held in Belarus on December 8, 1991, and invited other former republics of the Soviet Union to join, which many did.[29] To all intents and purposes, this ended the existence of the Soviet Union.

POST–SOVIET COOPERATIVE SECURITY

The collapse of the Soviet Union, a nuclear-armed superpower, created a new set of problems for cooperative security. Soviet nuclear weapons had been safeguarded by the mechanisms of a police state: restrictions on movements of people, well-guarded defense facilities, and secrecy. Much of that disappeared when the Soviet Union collapsed. Weapons themselves were still fairly well guarded, but fissile materials were relatively vulnerable to theft.

Senators Sam Nunn (D-GA) and Richard Lugar (R-IN) had the vision to call for American assistance to Russia in protecting vulnerable nuclear materials and in expediting the elimination of strategic nuclear delivery systems, called for in the START agreement. They succeeded by having legislation adopted in December 1991 by Congress that provided for such assistance to be taken from the US Defense Department budget. The defense secretary then was Dick Cheney, who was not happy about taking money from the budget he had proposed for other purposes. Despite this, the Bush I administration set up a process for implementing the Nunn-Lugar legislation. This consisted of negotiating with Russia, Belarus, Ukraine, and Kazakhstan on "umbrella agreements" that generally described the scope of the Nunn-Lugar agreement with each country and "implementing agreements" that spelled out what goods and services would be provided and under what conditions.

Major General William F. Burns, US Army (Ret.) was the first chief negotiator. I took over from him in March 1993 and served in that position through March 1994. During that year, our interagency negotiating team concluded over thirty agreements with Russia, Belarus, Ukraine, and Kazakhstan.

President Yeltsin's decision to continue the nuclear restraint talks with Reagan's next two successors yielded to a START II agreement despite opposition from Russian conservatives. President George W. Bush adopted neoconservative doctrines with regard to arms control, in particular, withdrawing from Nixon's 1972 Anti-Ballistic Missile Treaty. The result was that the START II agreement never entered into force.

Among other presidential decisions, the George W. Bush administration announced that preemption (effectively preventive war) was a necessary element of US deterrent strategy and blurred the distinction between nuclear and conventional warfare. In addition, it shifted the US nonproliferation doctrine away from Reagan's view that nuclear weapons were inherently evil to one in which the nature of the government that possessed them determined whether nuclear weapons were good or bad.

President George W. Bush's decision to withdraw from the US–Soviet Anti-Ballistic Missile Treaty had many consequences, not least the effect on Vladimir Putin's impressions of the future of US-Russian security cooperation. Vladimir Putin was president of the Russian Federation at the time and argued that the American decision to abandon restraints on ballistic missile defenses was a mistake. It is not hard to imagine his reaction when his views were essentially ignored.[30]

MOMENTUM LOST AND REGAINED
AND LOST AGAIN

President Nixon and his advisors had recognized that stability in strategic nuclear relations required restraints over both offensive and defensive nuclear forces. President George W. Bush rejected that view and also resisted the very idea that any negotiated restraints on nuclear forces were necessary to enhance stability in a post–Cold War world. In that spirit, his administration announced that it would accept a treaty commitment on strategic offensive forces only to ratify unilateral decisions already taken by the United States. And so there emerged from a brief negotiation between Russia and the United States a three-page agreement called "Treaty Between the United States of America and the Russian Federation on Strategic Offensive Reductions" that was constructed so as to expire on the same day the nuclear reductions were to be reached.[31]

President Obama tried to restore the momentum toward bilateral nuclear reductions that the Reagan-Gorbachev cooperation had created and that Bush I and Yeltsin had perpetuated. His speech in Prague, Czech Republic, in 2009 laid out an ambitious agenda, including working for a world without nuclear weapons.[32] His administration did succeed in negotiating a strategic nuclear forces treaty, New START, which restored the general framework for nuclear reductions that presidents Ronald Reagan and George H. W. Bush had created with the START agreement of 1991. New START was important not only for that reason but also because of the innovative approach to verification that it contained.[33] But after that, Vladimir Putin made it clear that no further reductions or even negotiations about reductions were possible while military threats to Russia remained unconstrained. Threats of concern to Moscow are:

- Long-range precision conventional weapons;
- Third-country nuclear weapons;
- US deployments of elements of a US ballistic missile defense system in Europe; and
- US insistence on maintaining US tactical nuclear weapons in Europe while asking for limits on Russian tactical nuclear weapons.

Other Russian specialists emphasize the nearly unilateral US approach to international conflict and relations as a key reason for Russia's disaffection with the West. Whether NATO expansion or invasion and regime change in Iraq or Libya after 9/11, or the previous decade's NATO actions in the former Yugoslavia, the United States is viewed by some as a renegade in international relations. President Putin delivered a speech at the 2007 Munich Security Conference that amounted to his declaration of complaints against Washington.[34] His own actions later in the annexations of Crimea and support for independence movements in Eastern Ukraine have locked Russia and the West into a confrontation that shows no signs of easing. In 2017, the prospects for deeper US-Russian reductions are bleak, pending major improvements in US-Russia relations.

Many of the states now possessing nuclear weapons are actively developing programs to upgrade nuclear warhead and delivery systems, some far more aggressively than others. So it is fair to say, as Yale professor Paul Bracken has written, that we are now well into "the second nuclear age."[35] Where it will stop, in terms of nuclear weapons programs by the current four nuclear-armed states that are nonmembers of the NPT, not to mention the five nuclear weapons states that are members, is anybody's guess. The more salient question may be: Unless the world can step back from the tipping point, how soon will nuclear weapons be used in conflict for the first time since 1945?

NOTES

1. Albert Einstein with Leo Szilard to President Franklin D. Roosevelt, August 2, 1939, in "The Manhattan Project: An Interactive History," *US Department of Energy*, https://www.osti.gov/opennet/manhattan-project-history/Events/1939 -1942/einstein_letter.htm.

2. Patrick Coffey, *American Arsenal: A Century of Waging War* (New York: Oxford University Press, 2013).

3. "Early Government Support—1939," *Atomic Heritage Foundation*, http://www.atomicheritage.org/history/early-government-support-1939.

4. Robert S. Norris, *Racing for the Bomb: General Leslie R. Groves, the Manhattan Project's Indispensable Man* (Hanover, NH: Steerforth Press, 2002). For a brief description, see http://www.americanscientist.org/bookshelf/pub/the-manhattan-projects-taskmaster.

5. "The Unlikely Pair," *Atomic Heritage Foundation*, http://www.atomicheritage .org/history/unlikely-pair.

6. Patrick Coffey, *American Arsenal: A Century of Waging War*.

7. Richard L. Garwin, "Living with Nuclear Weapons: Sixty Years and Counting," *Proceedings of the American Philosophical Society* 152, no.1 (March 2008), http://www.jstor.org/stable/pdf/25478469.

8. John Walsh, "A Manhattan Project Postscript," *Science* 212, no. 4501 (June 1981), http://www.jstor.org/stable/pdf/1686773.

9. Enrico Fermi, "The Development of the First Chain Reacting Pile," *Proceedings of the American Philosophical Society* 90, no. 1 (January 1946), http://www .jstor.org/stable/pdf/3301034.

10. "CP-1 Goes Critical," *US Department of Energy*, https://www.osti.gov/opennet/manhattan-project-history/Events/1942-1944_pu/cp-1_critical.htm.

11. Richard G. Hewlett, "Pioneering on Nuclear Frontiers: Two Early Landmarks in Reactor Technology," *Technology and Culture* 5, no. 4 (Autumn 1964), http://www.jstor.org/stable/pdf/3101216.

12. "Next Steps in Reducing Nuclear Risks," *Wall Street Journal* (March 6, 2013).

13. Garwin, "Living with Nuclear Weapons."

14. Wilson D. Miscamble, *The Most Controversial Decision: Truman, the Atomic Bombs, and the Defeat of Japan* (New York: Cambridge University Press, 2011).

15. Wilson D. Miscamble, *The Most Controversial Decision: Truman, the Atomic Bombs, and the Defeat of Japan*.

16. "Espionage and The Manhattan Project," *US Department of Energy*, https://www.osti.gov/opennet/manhattan-project-history/Events/1942-1945/espionage.htm.

17. "The Acheson-Lilienthal & Baruch Plans, 1946," *US Department of State*, https://history.state.gov/milestones/1945-1952/baruch-plans.

18. Gregg Herken, "'A Most Deadly Illusion': The Atomic Secret and American Nuclear Weapons Policy, 1945–1950," *Pacific Historical Review* 49, no. 1 (February 1980), http://www.jstor.org/stable/pdf/3639304.

19. For a summary of these agreements, see https://www.armscontrol.org/factsheets/USRussiaNuclearAgreementsMarch2010.

20. For the status of global nuclear inventories, specifically US versus Russian stockpiles, see https://www.icrc.org/en/international-review/article/nuclear-arsenals-current-developments-trends-and-capabilities.

21. "Strategic Arms Reduction Treaty I (START I)," *Arms Control Association*, https://www.armscontrol.org/treaties/strategic-arms-reduction-treaty-i; for details of the INF (Intermediate-Range Nuclear Forces) Treaty, see https://www.state.gov/t/avc/trty/102360.htm. For statements of the Presidential Nuclear Initiatives (PNI), see http://www.nti.org/analysis/articles/presidential-nuclear-initiatives/.

22. Rupert Cornwell, "Bush signs Nuclear Test Moratorium," *The Independent* (October 2, 1992), https://www.independent.co.uk/news/world/bush-signs-nuclear-test-moratorium-1555090.html. For the timeline of CTBT, see *Arms Control Association*, https://www.armscontrol.org/factsheets/Nuclear-Testing-and-Comprehensive-Test-Ban-Treaty-CTBT-Timeline.

23. "Treaty Between the United States of America and the Russian Federation on Strategic Offensive Reductions (The Moscow Treaty)," *US Department of State*, https://www.state.gov/t/isn/10527.htm.

24. "New START," *US Department of State*, https://www.state.gov/t/avc/newstart/.

25. "UN Votes to Outlaw Nuclear Weapons in 2017," *International Campaign to Abolish Nuclear Weapons*, http://www.icanw.org/campaign-news/un-votes-to-outlaw-nuclear-weapons-in-2017/. For full voting results of UN Resolution L.41, see http://www.icanw.org/campaign-news/results/.

26. Winston Churchill, "The Sinews of Peace" (speech, Westminster College, Fulton, MO, March 5, 1946), http://www.winstonchurchill.org/resources/speeches/1946-1963-elder-statesman/120-the-sinews-of-peace.

27. "Treaty Banning Nuclear Weapon Tests in the Atmosphere, in Outer Space, and Under Water," *US Department of State*, https://www.state.gov/t/isn/4797.htm.

28. Thomas C. Schelling and Morton H. Halperin, *Strategy and Arms Control*, New York: The Twentieth Century Fund, 1961.

29. The Commonwealth currently consists of Armenia, Azerbaijan, Belarus, Kazakhstan, Kyrgyzstan, Moldova, Russia, Tajikistan, Turkmenistan, Ukraine, and Uzbekistan. Both Turkmenistan and Ukraine are associate member states; Georgia withdrew its membership in 2008, *Commonwealth of Independent States*, http://www.cis.minsk.by.

30. President Putin spoke of this recently in explaining the need for more emphasis on nuclear offensive forces; he asserted that Russia must "strengthen the strategic nuclear forces . . . [to] develop missiles capable of penetrating any current and prospective missile defense systems." Max Seddon and Demetri Sevastopulo, "Putin and Trump Call for Stronger Nuclear Forces," *Financial Times* (December 22, 2016).

31. "Treaty Between the United States of America and the Russian Federation on Strategic Offensive Reductions (The Moscow Treaty)," *US Department of State*, https://www.state.gov/t/isn/10527.htm.

32. Paul Reynolds, "Assessing Obama's Nuclear Weapons Agenda," *BBC News* (April 14, 2010), http://news.bbc.co.uk/1/hi/8617687.stm.

33. "Nuclear Warhead Verification: A Review of Attribute and Template Systems," *Science and Global Security*, http://scienceandglobalsecurity.org/archive/sgs23jieyan.pdf.

34. Thom Shanker and Mark Landler, "Putin Says US Is Undermining Global Stability," (Russian president Vladimir Putin's speech at the International Security Conference in Munich), *The New York Times* (February 11, 2007), http://www.nytimes.com/2007/02/11/world/europe/11munich.html.

35. Paul Bracken, *The Second Nuclear Age: Strategy, Danger, and the New Power Politics* (New York: Henry Holt & Co., 2012).

TWO

Stepping Back from the Tipping Point

Every rational creature, finding itself on the brink of a disaster, first tries to get away from the brink and only then does it think about the satisfaction of its other needs.

—Andrei Sakharov

Looking back over the seven decades since atomic bombs were used in World War II, it seems that complacency about the possible use of these weapons in war is now the mood of the day to an extent not seen before. Stewardship of the planet requires us to act on the understanding that nuclear weapons today constitute one of the major existential threats to human society and our environment as we know them. Terrorist groups could be hugely empowered if they could acquire even one nuclear weapon. Reconciliation and resolution of conflicts are greatly complicated when competing nations possess nuclear weapons. Although nuclear proliferation has been limited, it has been occurring in unstable parts of the world. Changes in the international system, caused by globalization and rapid technological advances, mean that more chaotic relations than in the past decades are likely in store for us. All of this spells trouble.

WHAT IS A "TIPPING POINT?"

George Shultz, Henry Kissinger, William Perry, and Sam Nunn suggested in their first joint article in 2007 that the world was reaching a "tipping point" with respect to nuclear weapons.[1] In the context of their appeal for reducing and ultimately eliminating nuclear weapons, the term implied that a time was approaching when the international control of nuclear weapons would no longer be possible and the world would slip into a chaos with a nuclear war being the likely result.

My own take on the prospects and hopes for avoiding nuclear war is that a tipping point is difficult to discern until it is upon us. This makes

23

the exercise of statecraft aimed at creating the conditions for a world without nuclear weapons so essential and so difficult to do. Preventive diplomacy will be more effective than nuclear deterrence in preventing a nuclear war.

Alexander George, my mentor and a distinguished professor of political science at Stanford University, wrote about the qualities of peace, suggesting that a "stable peace" was one in which war had been excluded as a means of solving problems among nations. A "conditional peace" was one in which war was unlikely but nations had not excluded the possibility of war to solve their problems. A "precarious peace" was one in which nations were at peace but war could break out on short notice.[2]

Similar distinctions could be made among different forms of stability, the necessary precondition for peace. A "precarious stability" is seen very often in the natural world and that condition is said by scientists to be "metastable." This condition also exists in human affairs. An apparently calm and stable situation could be either stable or metastable and that is why tipping points are so hard to predict and why preventive diplomacy is the best way of avoiding them. By that, I mean efforts to resolve disputes and create ground rules among nations, also known as order.

A pile of sand or a mountainside covered with snow that is in a condition of precarious stability appears stable until a single grain of sand or a lone skier causes an avalanche. This tells us that a small input can create a massive change in a metastable system. So it was with Tunisia in 2010–2011. On December 17, 2010, a street vendor named Mohamed Bouazizi set himself on fire as an act of desperation and defiance in the face of prolonged and persistent bullying by city police as he sought to sell his produce in the streets of Tunis. He died on January 4, 2011, and the riots throughout Tunisia generated by this incident caused the resignation on January 14, 2011, of Tunisia's president, Zine El Abidine Ben Ali, who had presided over a relatively tranquil nation for twenty-three years. Tunisia's example led to protests in other Arab nations and to the general surge of rage against autocratic Arab rulers that became known as the Arab Spring.

Given the uncertain state of relations among three major nuclear weapons states—the United States, China, and Russia—could the stability that seems to exist among them in fact be a metastable condition? It is possible. The Middle East cannot be said to have become stable, despite the nuclear agreement with Iran and despite the relative calm created by the reassertion of autocratic power in most Arab nations. Civil war in Syria currently shows little sign of ending and this promotes a precarious stability elsewhere in the region. Northeast Asia is clearly in or is on the brink of being in a metastable condition. North Korea's rapid advances in nuclear and missile technologies have added to the tensions that already roil the region. South Asia definitely is in a metastable condition. Despite relative calm, military dispositions on both sides in the India-Pakistan confrontation can easily be misinterpreted by one side or the other. And this delicate situation is exacerbated by a bitter dispute over Kashmir, an unstable Afghanistan, and an active terrorist operation in Pakistan.

All this means that in each of these three regions, and possibly even in the China-Russia-United States system of nations, a small input—a nuclear accident, for example—could generate a very large response, including a nuclear war.

In nature, metastable conditions can change into stable conditions and this must be our goal in international relations. But what does the fact that the whole world is likely to become more chaotic over the next decade than it has been in many decades mean for the prospect that change will be in the direction of stability in human affairs? While the undisputed place of national governments as the prime movers and shakers in international politics is being questioned, they are still looked to by those they govern to solve problems. Notably, their people and the private organizations that identify with nations also expect governments to assure them a fundamental level of safety and security. Governments recently have interpreted the people's wishes as meaning they should act independently of other nations. If governments of major nations, seemingly under pressure from their people, give up on security cooperation with other nations, humanity will be in a poor position to prevent minor incidents from escalating out of control. That does not have to be our fate.

The threat we face demands that a greater sense of urgency should be devoted to the control of nuclear weapons than is now the case. I have worked closely with former US Secretary of State George Shultz, former Secretary of Defense William Perry, and the late nuclear physicist Dr. Sidney Drell over the past ten years at Stanford University's Hoover Institution. Our core project was called "A World Without Nuclear Weapons." The phrase became well known as a result of President Obama's unequivocal embrace of the idea in his first year in office. The UN Security Council also adopted this goal in its meeting on September 24, 2009, and added the mission of "creating the conditions for a world without nuclear weapons."[3] A remarkable number of other nations and national leaders also have supported the idea. The president of China spoke out in favor on January 18, 2017. UN Resolution L.14 was adopted by a very large majority of the world's nations in the fall of 2016. It authorized the negotiation of a treaty to ban nuclear weapons.[4]

When we began this project at Hoover, we had in mind the dramatic meeting between Ronald Reagan and Mikhail Gorbachev at Reykjavik in

1986—over thirty years ago. The two leaders spoke there in dead serious-ness of eliminating nuclear weapons. In 2006, those of us then at the Hoover Institution asked ourselves whether that idea could be rekindled and we organized several conferences to explore that possibility.

Many, perhaps all, of the participants in our conferences saw the world as teetering on the edge of a new and more perilous nuclear era. The developing situation, they thought, was not favorable to nuclear non-proliferation. But that was not all. New dangers that did not exist in the Cold War have heightened the risks posed by more nuclear weapons in more hands. These new dangers include international terrorism, well-organized nuclear black markets, and the rise of cyber attacks (both crimi-nal and state-sponsored), which would make the management of any future nuclear crisis even more difficult. Since those conferences took place, it is evident that global systemic change and nationalist backlash have further roiled the waters. The world seems to be moving toward a metastable and unstable condition, rather than away from one.

The Hoover conferences essentially ratified the view that linking imme-diate actions to strengthen the nuclear restraint regime with the long-term vision of eliminating nuclear weapons would both make the world a safer place and at the same time produce synergies that would encourage progress toward a world without nuclear weapons. The participants agreed that measures to provide greater safety to all of the world's people should be pursued with all the intensity the imminence of the threat required. In advocating the elimination of nuclear weapons, we all hoped to inspire that intensity and galvanize governments into action. We also thought of eliminating nuclear weapons not only as an eventual goal, but also as a compass that should guide current decision making. That seemed to be a possibility once, but not now, and the direction of travel needs to be reversed. This book will show how that could be done.

Sir Michael Quinlan, the late British strategist, wrote in his last book, *Thinking About Nuclear Weapons*:

> The longer possessor countries continue to act, or are thought to be acting, as though "eventual" meant something like "contemporaneously with the abolition of all evil in the world," the greater the danger that this element of the multi-part deal centred upon the NPT [Non-Proliferation Treaty] will cease to bear its load, with peril to the entire regime.[5]

When one considers the immense amounts of energy and resources that have been devoted to theories of nuclear deterrence as opposed to how little effort has been devoted to how to live without nuclear bombs and warheads, one must conclude that we have a lot of catching up to do.

SHOULD WE WANT TO ELIMINATE
NUCLEAR WEAPONS?

Secretary Shultz and his colleagues Henry Kissinger, William Perry, and Sam Nunn wrote, in their now-famous *Wall Street Journal* article in 2007, that "Deterrence continues to be a relevant consideration for many states with regard to threats from other states. But reliance on nuclear weapons for this purpose is becoming increasingly hazardous and decreasingly effective."[6] It is important to note that in this formulation, "deterrence" did not inevitably correspond to deterrence by the threat of using nuclear weapons. Deterrence will always be with us, but a nuclear component is not always necessary, even today.

Looking back at Cold War experiences, some other veterans of those days believe, implicitly or explicitly, that it is unthinkable that the United States should eliminate nuclear weapons, even if all other nations did so. This attitude tends to overlook the likelihood that the US-Soviet model of nuclear deterrence during the Cold War was unique and is not the template for other nuclear relationships.

Deterrence in a world with multiple powers possessing nuclear bombs and warheads will almost certainly not work as effectively or with the same assurance of success (in particular, avoiding misunderstanding or miscalculation) as the bilateral balance of terror achieved between the United States and the Soviet Union. And, it should be emphasized, even that fairly stable bilateral model brought the world very close to disaster.

I will make this point in personal terms.[7] On October 22, 1962, I was a Foreign Service Officer assigned temporarily to the US Delegation to the United Nations to try to advance the stalled nuclear test ban negotiations. US Ambassador Adlai Stevenson invited members of his delegation to join him in his office at the United Nations that evening to hear what President Kennedy would say to the nation, which had not then been divulged. What he announced was shocking. He said the Soviet Union had deployed missiles and bombers in Cuba capable of carrying nuclear warheads to targets in the United States and elsewhere in the Western Hemisphere. Kennedy's bottom line was: "It shall be the policy of this nation to regard any nuclear missile launched from Cuba against any nation in the Western Hemisphere as an attack by the Soviet Union on the United States, requiring a full retaliatory response upon the Soviet Union."[8]

Over the next days the crisis eased, but it was a close call—closer than we knew at the time.[9] The event underscores why we should want more time for decision making—much more time than current nuclear deployments encourage. And it underscores the advantage of having only two players in a crisis rather than several, as is now the case.

After the Cuban Missile Crisis, Harvard professor Thomas Schelling (later a Nobel Laureate) persuaded Walt Rostow, the chairman of the State Department's Policy Planning Council, and McGeorge Bundy, Kennedy's, and later Johnson's, National Security Advisor, to start a study on how a nuclear war could be ended once it had started. And so, in 1963, the National Security Council staff was directed by the highest authorities in the US government to examine the concept of management and termination of war with the Soviet Union. The work was done by a group called the Net Evaluation Subcommittee and its conclusions were reported in a Top Secret Limited Distribution report, now declassified.[10] As a member of the State Department's Policy Planning Council, I had been assigned to the mainly military team that wrote the report. This is what we said:

> The United States must always be prepared for the worst case, namely, that of a Soviet-initiated nation-killing attack: Vital to such a situation would be a high assurance of being able to destroy the USSR no matter what degree of surprise the Soviets might achieve. . . . In the event of a nation-killing attack, the implementation of a sophisticated response capability, attempts at war management in order to limit the total effects of war, or attempts to negotiate the termination of the war would have little chance of success. Any implementation of these concepts under such circumstances therefore must not be permitted to risk the degradation of our capability to destroy the Soviet Union.

This was the logic of mutual assured destruction (MAD). That's what a "full retaliatory response" implied.

Two decades after the Cuban near-miss, President Reagan not only said that a nuclear war could not be won and must never be fought he also advocated the elimination of nuclear weapons. He was strongly supported in this by Secretary of State George Shultz. Soviet general secretary, and later president, Mikhail Gorbachev, joined them in this vision. They were ahead of their times. Reagan was roundly criticized by the experts and some allies, notably British Prime Minister Margaret Thatcher, for daring to say this.

Nearly everyone agrees now, in 2017, that mutual assured destruction as a strategy is obsolete, but both Russia and the United States are still stuck in a version of the mutual assured destruction trap. The immediate threats each country faces are from terrorism, ethnic and sectarian conflicts, cyber warfare, asymmetric warfare, and illicit trade in nuclear materials. These threats cannot be deterred by the use of nuclear weapons.

When we hear the words "nuclear threat," our imagination conjures up images of mushroom clouds and radioactive ruins where cities once stood, as though the sun had touched the earth. Most of us assume that this image is so horrible that it will induce caution in national leaders who otherwise might be tempted to take risks in achieving their goals.

Risk assessment is highly subjective. Even if we assign a very low probability number to the possibility that at a given moment someone will not be deterred by the threat of nuclear devastation, when assessed over time, the probability of the use of nuclear weapons becomes unacceptably high.[11] If we add to that the possibility of accident or miscalculation, and then add to that the very real possibility of false signals being introduced into a crisis situation by hackers, then the odds are fairly high that nuclear weapons may be detonated at some point in the next several years. And this is an assessment that does not include the possibility that terrorists will be able to buy or steal a nuclear weapon and detonate it in a major city somewhere in the world. If the world were in a metastable condition when this occurred, a human catastrophe would be a near certainty.

The nuclear threat to humanity has received less attention than it should have in recent years. It still exists and the effects of even a very limited use in war of nuclear weapons would have global effects. Managing a nuclear war, once started, is a hypothetical possibility but it has never been tried, so it remains hypothetical and, in my view, highly suspect. The conclusion of the Net Evaluation Subcommittee cited above is a more realistic outcome.

Is there a defense? No, not really. An adequate defense is impossible against a large-scale nuclear attack with ballistic missiles despite billions of dollars spent over decades by the United States in the effort to solve that problem. Attacks by terrorist or rogue organizations can be prevented by maintaining strict control over access to bomb-making material and airtight custodial control over nuclear weapons. If those controls fail, most experts think that smuggling a nuclear bomb into the United States or some other technologically advanced nations would be relatively easy.

The imminence of the nuclear threat humanity faces today has been ignored. Among the reasons for complacency and a lack of urgency about this threat is the widespread belief that nuclear weapons can deter war. People look at the long peace among major nations since World War II and conclude that nuclear weapons therefore exercise a beneficial effect on interstate relations. There is no real proof for this belief and there is plenty of evidence that nuclear weapons have exacerbated relations between states and made disputes more difficult to resolve. See chapter 4 for more on this subject.

RESTRAINT MODELS TO CONSIDER IN FUTURE NEGOTIATIONS

The Cold War years saw many experiments in cooperative security that could be useful under current and projected circumstances. They include the following:

- *Nuclear weapons-free zones.* Several such zones already exist in various parts of the world: Africa, Latin America, Central Asia, and the South Pacific. These have reinforced decisions taken by nations in those regions to forgo nuclear weapons. Such zones have not yet been put into place in the Middle East, South Asia, and Northeast Asia because the political and security agreements that must necessarily accompany commitments to forgo nuclear weapons have seemed out of reach. That could change with leadership from global and regional powers.

- *Reciprocal actions and enhanced transparency.* The best example of reciprocal action is the Presidential Nuclear Initiative (PNI) of 1991–1992 taken by President George H. W. Bush, which resulted in the withdrawal of short-range nuclear weapons systems from forward deployment by the United States and led to Soviet redeployment of similar weapons from all other Soviet Republics to the Russian Republic.[12] The parallel actions created a more secure environment while the Soviet Union came apart and while some of the republics where strategic weapons were based accepted START obligations in a protocol signed at Lisbon. There are applications for such actions today as between Russia and the United States, India and Pakistan, and possibly as between North Korea and South Korea with respect to defense systems relevant to nuclear weapons. Mutual transparency mechanisms have been worked out in South America between Argentina and Brazil and also could be applied in other parts of the world.

- *The Strategic Offensive Reduction Treaty (SORT) model.* In 2002, presidents George W. Bush and Vladimir Putin agreed on a three-page treaty that committed each nation to reduce their stockpiles to an agreed level of deployed nuclear warheads.[13] Verification of these reductions was to be accomplished by a monitoring system already in place to confirm adherence to the START agreement that entered into force in 1994. There was no definition in the SORT agreement of how deployed warheads were to be counted. In testifying before the Senate, Secretary of State Colin Powell stated that warheads actually mounted on missiles—not those in reserve—would be counted as deployed.[14]

  This model of strategic nuclear reductions was a radical departure from all previous US-Soviet agreements in that the treaty itself lacked the detailed provisions for how to count warheads and what to do with nuclear delivery vehicles, not to mention the method of incorporating verification into the agreement. Nonetheless, this type of agreement may have its place in future nuclear arms control talks between the United States and Russia or in some regional efforts to begin the process of nuclear reductions.

There may be situations where this type of agreement would be useful because it amounts to a reduction in prompt-launch capabilities by removing warheads from missiles. This type of agreement might be applicable, for example, in the case of India and Pakistan, although some method of verification would have to be devised. Conceivably, a treaty like SORT could be considered in a US-China agreement.

WHAT MIGHT HAVE BEEN

The pioneering negotiations between Russia and the United States show how much can be done to limit and reduce the nuclear threat, while the present stalemate in nuclear negotiations between Moscow and Washington shows how vulnerable the process of reducing the nuclear threat is to political developments that seem more immediate and urgent. The Nuclear Test Ban Treaty is an iconic example of what an uphill battle it is to back away from the brink of a disaster. It should have been obvious that a treaty banning all nuclear testing in the 1950s or 1970s would have had the potential for turning humanity away from a nuclear arms race. It was "the road not taken." Why that happened will shed light on how the world might step back from the tipping point.

Five Crucial Years in the Test Ban Negotiations

The test ban negotiations were launched in 1958 in a spirit of hope, accompanied by a moratorium on explosive testing by the three parties in the talks: the United States, the Union of Soviet Socialist Republics, and the United Kingdom. Every year thereafter, from 1959 through 1963, when a Limited Test Ban Treaty was concluded, there were periods when the negotiations could easily have failed and others when the talks received a stimulus that moved them forward.

1959. New seismic data from US underground tests required a reassessment of the ability to detect decoupled nuclear tests. In 1958, Soviet and American scientists had agreed that underground testing could be monitored with seismic stations, but that finding was called into question. The negotiations were "on life support" during this period as critics of a comprehensive test ban treaty gained support in Congress and in parts of the Eisenhower administration.

1960. Active negotiations took place during Eisenhower's last year in office. A treaty banning atmospheric underwater and verifiable tests in space and under ground, coupled with a moratorium on underground tests, emerged as a serious possibility. It was derailed by the downing of an American U-2 reconnaissance aircraft by the Soviet Union over Sverdlovsk in the USSR.

1961. A disastrous year, 1961 was certainly the low point of the multiyear effort to negotiate a treaty. Khrushchev turned his back on test ban negotiations. Kennedy had to deal with a failed invasion of Cuba at the Bay of Pigs. A summit between Kennedy and Khrushchev in Vienna led to an acrimonious and unproductive exchange of views. Kennedy increased the defense budget. The Soviets and East Germans built the Berlin Wall. Finally, Khrushchev ended the test moratorium that Eisenhower had started in 1958 with a thermonuclear explosion of more than 50 megatons, the largest ever detonated. Both sides resumed testing.

1962. This year was notable primarily for the close brush with nuclear war during the Cuban Missile Crisis in October. But 1962 is also notable from the standpoint of test ban negotiations for the introduction, by the United States and the United Kingdom, of a Comprehensive Test Ban Treaty and of the Limited Test Ban Treaty in the form which later emerged, almost intact, from high-level talks in Moscow a year later. After the Cuban Missile Crisis, Khrushchev proposed three on-site inspections to monitor a comprehensive test ban and assented to private high-level talks in New York about the test ban.

1963. The first breakthrough in US-USSR nuclear restraint negotiations occurred this year. After the private talks in New York failed to break the impasse over the verification of the Comprehensive Test Ban Treaty, both sides engaged in a round of public diplomacy. On June 10, Kennedy delivered his great speech on peace, in which he included a declaration that the United States would refrain from testing nuclear weapons in the atmosphere.[15] He also announced that the Soviets had accepted a US-UK proposal to send a high-level mission to Moscow to discuss test ban issues. On July 2, Khrushchev spoke in Berlin and essentially accepted a test ban limited to three environments and excluding underground tests. His decision evidently was made in June 1963, and may have been prompted by the support for a test ban among Soviet scientists, including Andrei Sakharov. Other factors included the Sino-Soviet split and the brush with nuclear war over Cuba. The Moscow talks quickly endorsed the Limited Test Ban Treaty that had been introduced the year before in Geneva. The treaty was ratified later that year.[16]

This brief history shows how much events external to the actual negotiations affected the outcome and how important it is to foster a changed political relationship between adversaries.

No Room for Complacency: The Comprehensive Test Ban Treaty and Its Fate

It took from 1963 to 1996 for a Comprehensive Test Ban Treaty (CTBT) to be concluded:[17] that is, to expand the Limited Test Ban Treaty's prohibition of nuclear explosions in the atmosphere, oceans, and space to also include a ban on underground nuclear explosions. During that time, what had been essentially a tripartite negotiation grew into a large multilateral forum, the UN's Conference on Disarmament. President Clinton signed the CTBT in 1996 but the Senate refused to take it up for debate until 1999, by which time a majority of senators had coalesced in opposition to giving assent to ratification. Although President Clinton asked that the treaty be withdrawn from the floor of the Senate, his request was rejected and the Senate voted it down 51 to 48 with one abstention.

The next year, President Clinton and Secretary of State Madeleine Albright appointed former chairman of the joint chiefs, General John Shalikashvili, to review with individual senators what could be done to get the treaty ratified. I became his deputy. General Shalikashvili's report, submitted to President Clinton just before the end of his term of office, found that the treaty served US and international interests, and offered suggestions for congressional involvement in monitoring the treaty's implementation.[18] President Bush chose not to pursue ratification of the CTBT; in fact, his administration declared that it had no intention of seeking ratification.

President George H. W. Bush had declared a moratorium on all US nuclear weapons testing in 1992 at the request of the Senate. That moratorium was extended by President Clinton in 1993 and continued by President George W. Bush. The moratorium remains in effect in 2017. All nations possessing nuclear weapons, except North Korea, are currently observing their own version of a test moratorium. That includes the five permanent members of the UN Security Council, plus India and Pakistan. It is important to recognize that the several declared moratoriums are not in treaty form and that no agreed language unites the nations in a moratorium declaration.

After July 3, 1993, when President Clinton announced that the US nuclear test moratorium would be extended, other nations, at various times, announced their own voluntary, unilateral moratoriums on nuclear testing.[19] That created the moratorium regime that exists today: a series of unilateral, voluntary declarations. The international moratorium regime, we may hope, will be with us for a while even if the United States ratifies the Comprehensive Test Ban Treaty (CTBT) because some other key countries, including North Korea, also must ratify it and this will take time.

A ratified test ban treaty is far preferable to the current situation. A moratorium is supposed to be a *temporary cessation* of some activity, and that points to one of the flaws in the present arrangement: it is built on shifting sands. No one knows how long it will last, or even what it means.

The words "voluntary" and "unilateral" are associated with, and qualify the meaning of, a moratorium. And that also makes the point: the moratorium is not only temporary but it is also subject to any definition that a participating government wishes to give it. The statements that governments have made about their own individual moratoriums do not say they are abiding by the terms of the 1996 Comprehensive Test Ban Treaty.[20] They generally say they are observing a moratorium on nuclear testing. But the George W. Bush administration's stance even cast doubt on that. Here is a statement from 2007, nearing the end of that administration's time in office:

> The administration does not support the Comprehensive Test Ban Treaty and does not intend to seek Senate advice and consent to its ratification. There has been no change in the Administration's policy on this matter. . . . We cannot, however, provide guarantees regarding the voluntary moratorium.[21]

The Vienna Convention on the Law of Treaties has something to say about such a situation in article 18:

> A State is obliged to refrain from acts which would defeat the object and purpose of a treaty when:
> (a) It has signed the treaty or has exchanged instruments constituting the treaty subject to ratification, acceptance or approval, until it shall have made its intention clear not to become a party to the treaty; or
> (b) It has expressed its consent to be bound by the treaty, pending the entry into force of the treaty and provided that such entry into force is not unduly delayed.[22]

Despite this, during the Bush administration the United States continued to act in a way that conformed to the obligation to refrain from acts that would defeat the object and purpose of the treaty, and never officially informed the other signatory states of intentions not to become a party.[23]

President Obama announced in Prague on April 5, 2009 that his "administration will immediately and aggressively pursue US ratification of the Comprehensive Test Ban Treaty."[24] This statement left no doubt about the US obligation to refrain from acts which would defeat the object and purpose of the CTBT.

The absence of explosive testing by all nations except North Korea is not grounds for complacency. Reflect on how badly the 1958–1961 moratorium ended—with an atmospheric test by the Soviets of a 57-megaton hydrogen bomb, the largest nuclear weapon ever detonated by any nation. The climate of international opinion today and some improvements in interstate relations probably point to a less dramatic end to the moratorium regime, but the world is in a situation on this issue that borders on the metastable. It is clearly better to have some international regime that inhibits full-scale testing than none at all. But the antiproliferation effect of a moratorium is less than that which a treaty would provide. Nations are entitled to ask why they should sign on to a treaty that the United States will not ratify. Later in this book, I will discuss how some progress might be made towards a more stable test ban regime.

SUMMIT-LEVEL COMMITMENTS

Important commitments regarding US-Russian cooperation were signed with Russian President Vladimir Putin by President Bill Clinton and President George W. Bush. Had these commitments been carried out, a network of relations between the United States and Russia would have been established that, by now, would be fully operational. The integration of Russian and American security interests and organizations would be far advanced beyond the sorry state of relations today. Would this exercise in preventive diplomacy and order building have headed off Russian aggressive actions in Ukraine? Would Russia be cooperating with NATO today instead of seeing the alliance as the arch-enemy? No one can say for sure, but one can say that opportunities to take actions that would have provided for greater security for both nations were lost and the world is much worse off because of that. Perhaps some of these opportunities could be seized in the future.

Some of the more significant measures in the two declarations are listed below:

1. Strategic Stability Cooperation Initiative, a joint statement signed by presidents Clinton and Putin on September 6, 2000, in New York.[25]
   - Cooperate in the area of Theater Missile Defense.
   - Put into operation in Moscow the joint center for exchange of data to preclude the possibility of missile launches caused by a false missile attack warning.
   - Strengthen the Missile Technology Control Regime.
   - Promote a mutually beneficial technical exchange that will facilitate the implementation of the Comprehensive Test Ban Treaty after its entry into force.
   - Hold annual meetings of officials to coordinate their activities in ballistic missile defense.
   - Plan for a global missile nonproliferation approach.

2. Declaration of President George W. Bush and president Vladimir Putin signed in Moscow on May 24, 2002.[26]
   - Increase transparency in the area of missile defense, including the exchange of information on missile defense programs and tests.
   - Explore potential programs for the joint research and development of missile defense technologies.
   - Explore opportunities for intensified practical cooperation in missile defense for Europe.
   - Strengthen mutual confidence, expand transparency, share information and plans, and discuss strategic issues of mutual interest through the mechanism of a group chaired by the Foreign Ministers and Defense Ministers of Russia and the United States.

The declaration by presidents Clinton and Putin was essentially ignored by the administration of President George W. Bush when it took power in the United States in January 2001. President Bush considered that the end of the Cold War brought with it a new relationship with Russia, which made the nuclear agenda of previous administrations obsolete. This had been the view promoted by the neoconservative movement for several years.

The declaration of presidents Bush and Putin revealed a shared interest in consultations on missile defenses. However, President Bush's 2001 announcement that the United States was withdrawing from the Anti-Ballistic Missile (ABM) Treaty meant that little was ever done to implement the planned cooperative actions in ballistic missile defense that the Joint Declaration had announced.

PRESIDENT OBAMA'S AGENDA

The state of party politics in the United States bears some responsibility for the unfortunate indifference to the implementation of what could have been serious preventive diplomacy programs. A new president entering office adopts the "not invented here" attitude and moves on to his own agenda.

Something similar happened in the Obama administration. Encouraged by the joint statements of Shultz, Kissinger, Perry, and Nunn that supported "a world without nuclear weapons," Obama made their cause his own. In a landmark speech in Prague, Czech Republic, on April 5, 2009, early in his first year in office, the president stated "clearly and with conviction America's commitment to seek the peace and security of a world without nuclear weapons."

President Obama cited several near-term nuclear actions that he wanted to achieve. These became known as the "Prague agenda." The first was a "New Strategic Arms Reduction Treaty" with the Russians.[27] Obama's negotiating team succeeded in negotiating the "New START" treaty that created an innovative verification system, and mandated a modest reduction in strategic nuclear weapons. It encountered fierce opposition in the Senate, but with the help of several Republican senators, it received the requisite two-thirds vote. The treaty was ratified on February 2, 2011, after receiving a favorable vote for ratification by the US Senate by a vote of 71 to 26.

The other proposed actions were:

- US ratification of the Comprehensive Test Ban Treaty;
- A treaty to verifiably end the production of fissile materials for use with nuclear weapons;
- More resources and authority to strengthen international inspections and more consequences for countries caught breaking the rules of the NPT or trying to leave the NPT without cause;
- A new framework for civil nuclear cooperation, including an international nuclear fuel bank;
- US engagement with Iran regarding nuclear weapons;
- A new international effort to secure all vulnerable nuclear material around the world within four years;
- Work to turn efforts such as the Proliferation Security Initiative (PSI) and the Global Initiative to Combat Nuclear Terrorism (GICNT) into durable international institutions; and
- A global Nuclear Security Summit (NSS) hosted by the United States within a year.

COMPLACENCY IS A RECIPE FOR DISASTER

The president had some major successes in implementing the Prague agenda. New START and four productive Nuclear Security Summits constitute a substantial legacy by any measure. The Iran nuclear accords were another success. Some progress was made in ensuring the availability of nuclear fuel. The rest of the agenda met the same fate as the Clinton-Putin declaration and the Bush-Putin declaration: valuable ideas, but little or no progress. That will almost certainly continue to be the story unless and until public opinion, in the United States especially but also elsewhere in the world, begins to pressure world leaders to accord nuclear constraints a much higher priority than they have been given to date.

President Obama's frustrating experience in implementing his Prague agenda shows that even those limited steps he embraced are hard to achieve absent public support for the intense, persistent effort that cooperative security requires. There are currently not enough votes in the US Senate to guarantee the ratification of the Comprehensive Nuclear Test Ban Treaty (CTBT). Achieving an agreed multilateral halt to the production of fissile material for use in weapons has been impossible even to talk about, thanks to the determined opposition of Pakistan. Both of these "initiatives," by the way, have been on the United States' to-do list since I first sat at a negotiating table with a Soviet delegation sixty years ago.

Why has it been so difficult to do these relatively simple things, and what does this tell us about the goal of a world free of nuclear weapons? First, it shows that treaties on cooperative security are inherently difficult to negotiate in an adversarial relationship. The huge reduction in global inventories of nuclear weapons since 1986 was the result not only of improved relations between the United States and Russia but also of reluctance to spend so much money on nuclear weapons. Both conditions appear to be reversed as of this writing.

SHOULD THE WORLD STOP WORRYING AND LEARN TO LIVE WITH THE BOMB?

That is the argument made by many nuclear "experts," who believe that eliminating nuclear weapons is impractical and undesirable. That would be a truly fatal mistake. Escaping a nuclear catastrophe will require a greater awareness than generally exists in the world of 2017; today's security environment has made reliance on nuclear deterrence a risky business. Consider what has happened since the end of the Cold War:

- The United States and Russia have returned to the habit of deep distrust and open hostility.
- Substate entities have shown themselves to be interested in and capable of inflicting mass casualties. If they could buy or steal a nuclear weapon, they would use it.
- India and Pakistan have built nuclear arsenals and have positioned their armed forces in ways that make nuclear war between them a serious possibility.
- North Korea has built the infrastructure for a nuclear weapons program and is testing missile systems, including submarines, to deliver nuclear warheads. There is nothing that prevents it from continuing to add nuclear weapons to its arsenal.
- The bipolar nuclear structure of the Cold War has been replaced by a complex structure distinguished by three global confrontations—in China, Russia, and the United States—and three regional

confrontations—in the Middle East, South Asia, and Northeast Asia. Opportunities for miscalculations abound.

- Science and technology have produced new weapons systems, including drones and cyber warfare, which make the practice of nuclear deterrence even more risky than it was during the Cold War. False signals, difficult to trace, will complicate a murky situation.

The premise that nuclear weapons prevent war or conditions that could lead to war is not demonstrably true, as Cold War and post–Cold War history bear out. Humanity does seem to be less inclined to violence now than in earlier times. Is this attributable to the presence of nuclear weapons? *The Better Angels of our Nature*, the widely praised book by Steven Pinker on the decline of violence, does not list nuclear deterrence as one of the six main causes of this decline.[28] According to Pinker, there is little evidence that the long peace can be credited to the threat of nuclear annihilation. In any case, the US-Soviet experience of the Cold War cannot be assumed to apply in very different situations where rivals harboring animosities rooted in years of hatred live right next door to each other and have territorial claims against each other.

Shultz, Kissinger, Perry, and Nunn asked in an article published on March 7, 2011: "Does the world want to continue to bet its survival on continued good fortune with a growing number of nuclear nations and adversaries globally?"[29] They had in mind that while the incidence of errors in nuclear operations is low, the risks are extremely high. In a book edited by George Shultz and Sidney Drell entitled *The Nuclear Enterprise*, it was reported that thirty-two "Broken Arrow" incidents involving US nuclear weapons were recorded between 1950 and 1980.[30] Several serious incidents have been reported in the US press recently. It would be foolish to entrust the well-being and safety of humanity to the premise that nuclear deterrence can go on forever without any chance of mistakes or errors in judgment.

Fundamentally, the world has to shake off the widespread impression that nuclear weapons kept the world relatively safe during the Cold War and can therefore continue to keep us safe now. There were many reasons that US-USSR relations were relatively stable, of which the nuclear standoff may have been one. But nuclear weapons were, and are, the gravest threat to the survival of nations and to civilization as we know it. National leaders need to consider how the principle of proportionality in warfare, a part of just war doctrine, could, in practice, be applied when an attack with even one nuclear weapon would produce enormous damage and the retaliatory nuclear attack would likely strike at a number of targets considered "threatening." To depend on nuclear deterrence indefinitely into the future, especially when other means of deterrence are available, is foolhardy.

The Obama administration declared that "the fundamental role of US nuclear weapons, which will continue as long as nuclear weapons exist, is to deter nuclear attack on the United States, our allies, and partners." But the administration also announced that "there remains a narrow range of contingencies in which US nuclear weapons may still play a role in deterring a conventional attack or an attack with chemical or biological weapons against the United States or its allies and partners."[31] The Obama administration said that it would work to establish conditions for a US policy which would state that "deterring nuclear attack is the sole purpose of nuclear weapons." That did not happen during President Obama's term of office but the goal was a noble one. Perhaps another administration will be more successful.

Notes

1. George Shultz, Henry Kissinger, William Perry, and Sam Nunn, "A World Free of Nuclear Weapons," *The Wall Street Journal* (January 4, 2007).

2. J. E. Goodby, *Europe Undivided: The New Logic of Peace in US-Russia Relations* (Washington, DC: United States Institute of Peace Press, 1998). Foreword by Alexander L. George.

3. "Historic Summit of Security Council Pledges Support for Progress on Stalled Efforts to End Nuclear Weapons Proliferation," *United Nations*, http://www.un.org/press/en/2009/sc9746.doc.htm.

4. For a discussion of this issue, see Edward Ifft, "A Challenge to Nuclear Deterrence," *Arms Control Today/Arms Control Association* (March 2017).

5. Michael Quinlan, *Thinking About Nuclear Weapons: Principles, Problems, Prospects* (New York: Oxford University Press, 2009), 155.

6. George Shultz, Henry Kissinger, William Perry, and Sam Nunn, "A World Free of Nuclear Weapons," *The Wall Street Journal* (January 4, 2007).

7. The following discussion of the Cuban Missile Crisis and the Net Evaluation Subcommittee's study of war management and termination is adapted from an article I wrote for the *Foreign Service Journal* (February 2013): 31–32.

8. President John F. Kennedy, "Radio and Television Report to the American People on the Soviet Arms Buildup in Cuba," October 22, 1962, https://www.jfk library.org/Asset-Viewer/sUVmCh-sB0moLfrBcaHaSg.aspx.

9. In particular, the United States did not know that nuclear warheads were already present in Cuba, such that should the US have attacked the missile sites—as advocated by key military leaders—atomic war would have been almost inevitable. Another close call involves a Soviet officer countermanding his submarine captain's order to use nuclear munition against threatening US naval forces.

10. 1964 report prepared by the Net Evaluation Subcommittee (NESC) of the

National Security Council, https://www.cia.gov/library/readingroom/docs/
CIA-RDP80B01676R000300180007–5.pdf.

11. I thank professor emeritus Martin Hellman, Stanford University, for this
insight. See, in particular, his "How Risky is Nuclear Optimism?" *Bulletin of the
Atomic Scientists*, 67(2), 47–56, 2011.

12. See endnote 21 of chapter 1.

13. "Treaty Between the United States of America and the Russian Federation
on Strategic Offensive Reductions (The Moscow Treaty)," *US Department of State*,
https://www.state.gov/t/avc/trty/127129.htm.

14. US Congress, Senate, Statement of Hon. Colin L. Powell, Secretary of State,
Hearings before the Committee on Foreign Relations, 117th Congress (2nd Session,
July 9, 17, 23, and September 12, 2002).

15. John F. Kennedy, "Commencement Address at American University, June
10 1963," https://www.jfklibrary.org/Asset-Viewer/BWC7I4C9QUmLG9J6I8oy
8w.aspx.

16. 1963 Limited Test Ban Treaty (LTBT), https://www.jfklibrary.org/JFK/
JFK-in-History/Nuclear-Test-Ban-Treaty.aspx.

17. "Comprehensive Nuclear Test-Ban Treaty (CTBT)," *US Department of State*,
https://www.state.gov/t/avc/c42328.htm.

18. "Shalikashvili Addresses Test Ban Treaty Concerns in New Report," *US
Department of State*, http://www.nti.org/media/pdfs/210.pdf?_=1316621538.

19. Here is a list of countries with the dates they signed and ratified a nuclear
test moratorium, https://www.ctbto.org/the-treaty/status-of-signature-and-rati
fication/.

20. For a history of the nuclear test moratorium see "Comprehensive Nuclear-
Test-Ban Treaty: Background and Current Developments," by Mary Beth D. Niki-
tin, *Congressional Research Service* (September 1, 2016).

21. Aiden Warren, *Prevention, Pre-emption and the Nuclear Option: From Bush to
Obama (Routledge Studies in US Foreign Policy)*, 1st ed. (Abingdon-on-Thames, UK:
Routledge, 2011).

22. Vienna Convention on the Law of Treaties (Vienna: United Nations, 1969),
available from https://treaties.un.org/doc/Publication/UNTS/Volume%201155
/volume-1155-I-18232-English.pdf.

23. I am obliged to Dr. Edward Ifft, Department of State, for this confirmation.

24. http://obamawhitehouse.archives.gov/the-press-office/remarks-
president-barack-obama-prague-delivered

25. "Strategic Stability Cooperation Initiative Between the United States of
America and Russian Federation Text of the Implementation Plan," *Federation of
American Scientists*, https://fas.org/nuke/control/abmt/text/090600js.htm.

26. "Joint Declaration on the New Strategic Relationship," *US Department of
State*, https://www.state.gov/t/avc/trty/127129.htm#13.

27. "Treaty Between the United States of America and the Russian Federation
on Measures for the Further Reduction and Limitation of Strategic Offensive
Arms," Prague, April 8, 2010, *US Department of State*, https://www.state.gov/
documents/organization/140035.pdf.

28. Steven Pinker, *The Better Angels of Our Nature: Why Violence Has Declined*
(New York: Viking, 2011).

29. George Shultz, Henry Kissinger, William Perry, and Sam Nunn, "Deterrence in the Age of Nuclear Proliferation," *Nuclear Threat Initiative (NTI)*, March 7, 2011, http://www.nti.org/analysis/opinions/deterrence-age-nuclear-proliferation/.

30. Sidney Drell and George Shultz, *The Nuclear Enterprise* (Stanford, CA: Hoover Institution Press, 2012).

31. "Nuclear Posture Review Report, April 2010," *US Department of Defense*, https://www.defense.gov/Portals/1/features/defenseReviews/NPR/2010_Nuclear_Posture_Review_Report.pdf.

THREE

Nationalism, Globalism, and Technology

There are seasons, in human affairs, of inward and outward revolution, when new depths seem to be broken up in the soul, when new wants are unfolded in multitudes, and a new and undefined good is thirsted for.

—William Ellery Channing

CHALLENGES TO COOPERATION AMONG NATIONS: THE PERMANENT REVOLUTION

It is not entirely coincidental that a downward spiral in security cooperation between Russia and the Western democracies has occurred over the past decade just as two transformative and disruptive developments gathered force. First, technology created powerful new tools for giving citizens a direct voice in their own affairs to a degree that they never had before. Social media have become instruments for organizing public opinion, often challenging established modes of governance. President Putin has believed for several years that the United States has used this as a tool to foment unrest. Putin implicitly accused Washington of inciting permanent revolution in a press conference in The Hague in 2004 and in a speech in February 2005.[1]

Second, global economic integration gave international corporations, mainly Western and Chinese, a powerful position in the global economy, giving them an advantage in shaping a new international system. Russia has not succeeded in joining the global economy on an equal footing with the Western nations or China. Still dependent on oil and gas exports, Russia's economy has been damaged by relatively low oil and gas prices.

The rapid globalization of national economies has been aided and abetted by advanced technologies that are spreading around the world, disrupting labor markets and depriving many regions of income-producing manufacturing plants. Challenges to the supremacy of the nation-state on the international chessboard and to people's self-identification have

43

arisen from these sudden developments, and this has led to a renewal of anti-foreign, nationalistic impulses in many advanced countries, the United States and European nations among them. The British vote to leave the European Union (Brexit) was one major demonstration of this mood in the Western democracies; the US presidential election of 2016 was another. Others arose in Europe as populist parties gained support in several Western and Central European nations.

The net effect of all these developments has been to render US–Russian security cooperation more difficult. And since cooperation between adversaries is essential for cooperative security agreements such as limits on nuclear weapons, it is arguable that global change, and the backlash against it that is now so visible, have become contributing factors in the inability of humanity to back away from the nuclear tipping point. Meanwhile, policy decisions in most of the states that possess nuclear weapons are leading to the modernization of their nuclear delivery systems and to the expansion of nuclear weapons arsenals in some of these nations.

Hans Kristensen and Robert Norris put it this way:

> The United States, Russia, and the United Kingdom are reducing their warhead inventories, but the pace of the reductions is slowing, compared with the past 25 years. France and Israel have relatively stable inventories, while China, Pakistan, India, and North Korea are enlarging their warhead inventories. All the nuclear weapon states continue to modernize their remaining nuclear forces and appear committed to retaining nuclear weapons for the foreseeable future.[2]

Global changes in the international system are not by themselves the principal causes of renewed competition and diminished cooperation in restraining nuclear weaponry. But cooperation between adversaries in the geopolitical sphere, both globally and regionally, has become more difficult to achieve in the chaotic environment that now exists. Governments have had the option, so far, of acting independently of the rules of the game that are gradually being put in place by the forces of the global economy and by new technologies because the price to be paid has not been judged to be excessive and the advantages of autonomy are superficially appealing.

Existential threats to humanity should attract the attention of the public, and social media could empower citizens to insist on the creation of new ways to meet these challenges. The problem has been that nations are divided over how to respond to these challenges, even while agreeing on the gravity of the threats.

Capacity building, that is, creating machinery for managing cooperative security, is key to overcoming differences in responding to existential threats. Rolling back the threat of nuclear devastation will require improved national and international governance; building the capacity to achieve this goal should enjoy broad public support. The task should be nonideological and it can be a practical, problem-solving, nonpartisan matter for governments. Success in this area might also show what could be possible in areas like climate change and pandemics. The opposite may also be true; that is, building the capacity to make headway fighting CO_2 emissions may show what could be accomplished in limiting and reducing the threat of nuclear weapons.

Global integration really should provide an impetus to progress in cooperative security. Why? Because, properly managed, the integration of national economies creates wealth, which adds to the well-being of all citizens, if equally shared. The effect of the comfort level of citizens on their willingness to support international agreements is not clear, but a generally unhappy and dispirited populace has led to nationalistic and aggressive impulses time after time.

Polling done in Great Britain in connection with Brexit showed a generational gap between young people, who wanted Britain to remain in the European Union, and older people, who voted to leave the European Union.[3] This was not just because of differences in employment possibilities but also because young people felt comfortable with the cosmopolitan environment that membership in the European Union brought to Britain, especially to urban areas in the south of England.

In England, the displacement of workers from industries that had failed, either because of technological changes or because comparative production advantages had passed to lower-wage nations, created a backlash against what the European Union offered, magnified by an influx of EU citizens into Britain. The anger of the workers was not lessened by the EU subsidies pumped into depressed zones. A study in the United States of voters supporting Donald Trump showed that the major factor affecting their discontent with their lot in life was how they viewed themselves relative to their parents' generation.[4] "Downwardly mobile" people were more likely to vote for Trump than those who made less money but saw themselves as upwardly mobile. What this suggests is that simply providing economic support or job training to depressed regions will not be sufficient to change public attitudes. A sense of equity has to be part of the response, and alternative means of gainful employment should be put in place to ease the adjustment to a different economy.

NATIONALISM, GLOBALISM, AND WORLD ORDER

The universal versus the particular has been a recurring theme in the human experience: the family versus the village, the village versus the nation, the nation versus other nations and, in Europe, versus the church. Now we see this phenomenon manifested in states versus regional and global institutions because the rapid pace of globalization and technological change has made the inevitable tension between the local and the universal more difficult to absorb and to dissipate.[5]

In contemporary times, the terms *nationalism* and *globalization* are used to describe the opposing poles, although the ideas are complementary because neither states nor a global economy can carry the whole burden of sustaining a world order. The two terms also include an array of meanings specific to political circumstances. In a polarized political environment, *nationalism* means that broadly shared economic, historical, and cultural experiences are used, typically with leadership from above, to mobilize public opinion in favor of policies that support autonomy, resistance to external influences, and reluctance to cooperate with other nations. In the same context, *globalization* refers to an economy in which business interests maximize profits by operating across borders, typically to reduce labor costs, and where the principle of comparative advantage results in "creative destruction" of manufacturing facilities in one country and the rise of new production facilities to take advantage of lower cost production wherever that can be found.

These two images do not reflect the real economic situation and there are generational differences of view, as well. An important element of globalization is a growing body of people, especially younger people, having a stake in their participation in an international economy and through the direct linkages available to them through the Internet. For older people in long-established industries, this is not the case. This phenomenon was quite apparent in the UK vote on Brexit.

The classic work of Hedley Bull, *The Anarchical Society: A Study of Order in World Politics*, provides a useful context for thinking about the institutional, order-building implications of the changes brought about by technology and global economic integration, and the backlash to both.[6] Professor Bull wrote that:

> The Kantian or universalist tradition . . . takes the essential nature of international politics to lie not in conflict among states . . . but in the trans-national social bonds that link the individual human beings who are the subjects or citizens of states.[7]

So far, so good: in the age that is now emerging, for the first time in history, it is possible to have "trans-national social bonds" of a more intimate and direct type than was technically achievable in earlier stages of history. But Bull also cites Kant's conclusion that moral imperatives "enjoin not coexistence and cooperation among states but rather the overthrow of the system of states and its replacement by a cosmopolitan society."[8] For the foreseeable future the administrative energy and coherence needed to drive cooperative security efforts very likely will remain in the hands of national governments. This is because national sentiments are powerful in most nations and governance will remain based on a social compact between national governments and the people they govern.

Practical and binding efforts to deal with existential threats will be the province of governments, aided and abetted by well-informed publics, probably within the framework of a global coalition of nations. Regional intergovernmental organizations and the powerful private companies that dominate the global economy may share the burden of sustaining cooperative security with governments, but national governments will dominate cooperative security programs. This is almost certain to be the model for cooperative security measures in the field of nuclear weaponry.

Intergovernmental mechanisms will be created to monitor nuclear reductions and related activities. This kind of capacity building ought to become one of the main aims of national governments in several fields of cooperative security. Whether a nationalist backlash will overwhelm the sense of self-preservation that ordinarily would create a momentum toward international cooperation remains to be seen.

What kind of world order might evolve in the coming decades? Hedley Bull considered alternatives to the contemporary states system in *The Anarchical Society*. One of the alternatives he described was "a new medievalism." By this he meant "a modern and secular equivalent of the kind of universal political organization that existed in Western Christendom in the Middle Ages." It sounds retrogressive or, more charitably, like going back to the future to speak of neo-medievalism, with its images of inquisitions and intolerance. But strip off the historical baggage and think only of the political structure of the medieval era and then compare it with the present scene. Surprisingly, it does appear that the international system may have been moving toward a structure that bears some resemblance to the medieval system. Ironically, when Hedley Bull tried to explain, forty years ago, what the United Kingdom would look like in a neo-medieval system, it came close to the exaggerated vision of a nation under siege that proponents of Brexit used in 2016 to make the case for leaving the European Union:

> If modern states were to come to share their authority over their citizens, and their ability to command their loyalties, on the one hand with regional and world authorities, and on the other hand with sub-state or sub-national authorities, to such an extent that the concept of sovereignty ceased to be applicable, then a neo-medieval form of universal political order might be said to have emerged.[9]

Neo-medievalism is a long way off if Hedley Bull's definition is the metric, but once the current chaos is behind us, a plausible international system might look something like the tiered structure of medieval Europe. In such a system, power sharing between public and private authorities would be desirable and probably expected because mutual interest would require it. Even in a power-sharing system like this, national governments are likely to be the dominant partners. So long as nation-states retain the allegiance of their citizens, their governance is likely to be more coherent and decisive than any other contenders for global authority.

National governments will not always have the last word. Shared or pooled sovereignty comes to mind when most of the American computer industry refuses to allow the federal government to have backdoor access to encrypted messages citizens send over smartphones, or when we see an artificial intelligence industry group organizing to set up their own rules of behavior lest governments do it for them.[10] If an integrated global economy persists into the future, which is likely, then private companies and regional and global organizations would want to share with national governments some of the decision-making responsibility, arguing that this would yield results more in line with a demand for growing prosperity and less wasteful competition. The major nations might successfully resist this, but a power-sharing system probably would appeal to most nations.[11]

TECHNOLOGICAL ENGINES OF CHANGE

From mundane conveniences to what Farhad Manjoo calls "globe-shaking power," many of the familiar applications of information technology have had dramatic effects, which almost certainly were not predicted, probably not foreseeable, and therefore unintended.[12] People tend to take these innovations for granted as a convenience and not think much about them, but a brief survey of some of the routine consequences of these innovations will suggest how profound these applications of information technology have really been.

> *The Internet.* The physical basis for this life-changing technology is the World Wide Web, which conveys an image in keeping with its consequences. Originally conceived as a means of communications within a community of scientists and engineers conducting research for the US Defense Department's Advanced Research Projects Agency (DARPA), the Internet now instantaneously connects billions of people around the globe, at very low cost, permitting cross-border linkages, including images as well as oral and written communications,

on a scale never before seen. Although encryption and passwords are now commonplace, the wall of privacy around each private citizen has eroded rapidly.

The Cloud. This innovation multiplies by many times the data storage capacity of individual computers. It empowers citizens by giving them the equivalent of a more powerful computer.

Big Data. This term refers to the digital information, including personal information, which is now collected in vast quantities and stored in the Cloud, where it is used for commercial purposes. It also raises privacy issues because it enables companies and governments to track the activities of individuals in frightening detail.

Mobile Computers. Smartphones, Periscope, and streaming are now so widely available that major businesses have sprung up to exploit the markets they have made possible. They have recorded demonstrations in the US House of Representatives and scenes of violence in the streets of American cities. These devices not only permit two-way communications from mobile bases but also furnish information services that were available to only a privileged few not many years ago. These devices are the essential enablers of all that the information revolution has made possible.

Social Media. This catchall term was originally intended to convey the idea that "the media" is no longer confined to institutions that provide information to the public but, instead, is potentially in the hands of every citizen. These applications, including Facebook and Twitter, quickly have become the source of news, generally only lightly filtered by editors or checked for facts, for millions of people.[13] They are the means by which populations are mobilized behind political or economic goals. To a large extent, public opinion is shaped today, including in popular elections, by social media, which is likely to become increasingly influential in the future. A survey conducted by Pew Research Center shows that nearly two-thirds of the participants aged 18 to 29 affirmed that social media was the most helpful source of information on the 2016 presidential election.[14]

Hacking. This phenomenon has become central to espionage and warfare as well as to theft, intimidation, and to the US electoral process. Hacking has important advantages for those who practice or encourage it: its perpetrators are hard to trace and effective deterrence or retaliation is hard to come by. It can be a profitable business enterprise. Controlling it or even channeling it in one direction or another is almost impossible. In a world where governments find it difficult to monopolize the instruments of power, hacking is one of the prime challenges to governmental and corporate authority and is also one of the weapons that governments themselves can use to subvert other governments.[15]

Search Engines. If "knowledge is power," a proposition that seems truer than ever today, search engines are key tools in the acquisition of power. Governments worry that search engines and the uses to which they are put can distort economic behavior. For citizens who are eager to learn how to build a bomb or develop three-dimensional capabilities for manufacturing guns, an efficient search engine is essential. For governments eager to shut off subversive information, managing or eliminating search engines becomes an imperative. Facebook engineers reportedly have been working on software to permit its users to suppress certain types of messages.[16]

Artificial Intelligence. This refers to machines that can sense their environment, learn by trial and error, solve problems, and take action. Artificial intelligence has been a dream of Silicon Valley engineers for many years. Recently, there have been significant breakthroughs, beginning with dramatic advances in voice recognition and language translation, and many more are on the horizon, including self-driving cars and trucks, which portend further disruption of workplaces worldwide.

Robotics. Robots, empowered by the advances in artificial intelligence, can be an awesome tool for performing tasks formerly requiring human beings. Rapid progress is being made in introducing robots into many areas of advanced economies. A recent study suggests that robots will take hold more gradually than some fear, but they are bound to have a major impact on the types of jobs available in the future.[17]

SOCIETAL IMPACT OF TECHNOLOGICAL INNOVATIONS

The effect of technology on society has been studied and discussed at least since the nineteenth century. In our time, as in the past, technology is changing economies and revolutionizing how people make their living. Although the history of applying new technologies to industry, health care, communications, agriculture, architecture, energy, and other major sectors of society shows positive and mostly anticipated results, there have been unintended consequences. Typically, these have been manageable byproducts of overwhelmingly beneficial improvements in human life. Even the most dubiously beneficial product of technology, the atom bomb, has been seen as the cause of peace among the world's major nations.

How will history view the consequences of the revolution in information technology, many of which were unintended? The 2016 US presidential elections offered some insights on this issue, as Facebook, Twitter, and Google found themselves being criticized for providing platforms for "fake news" and as Russian-sponsored hackers leaked private emails from the Democratic National Committee and the chairman of Hillary Clinton's campaign. The total effect on societies of the information revolution has yet to be realized, but already, the impact appears to have been significantly disorienting. Nearly fifty years ago, Alvin Toffler wrote the book *Future Shock*.[18] As he put it, he "coined the term 'future shock' to describe the shattering stress and disorientation that we induce in individuals by subjecting them to much change in too short a time." Toffler wrote that the *rate* of change "has implications quite apart from, and sometimes more important than, the *direction* of change."

When Toffler wrote this book, technological change had not achieved the momentum it now has, and the pace of that change is accelerating. The 2016 US presidential election was described as a "change election," and clearly it was, at several levels. At its most fundamental level, the results reflected a demand not only for changes that citizens wanted, but also a reaction to changes that came too fast for them to absorb and which made a viable adaptation to change almost impossible. Although trade agreements became the focus of public anger, technological changes almost certainly played an even greater role.

Because of automation, the labor-capital equation has been shifting to the advantage of capital and also to the advantage of highly skilled workers; in the process, this has contributed to income inequality. Technology is making production more efficient with fewer workers. That trend will continue and probably accelerate as artificial intelligence and robotics come into general use. This will make offshoring less interesting for American companies that rely heavily on robotics for production but this will not necessarily be a job-creating development.

Toffler argued that the introduction of new technologies should be controlled so that their effects on humanity could be judged before being let loose on society. In this way, the tempo of technological change could be moderated so as to forestall future shock. That has not happened, nor is it likely to. No major element of advanced societies has demanded it.

Luddites in nineteenth-century England agitated for a more equal balance in the distribution of the wealth generated by new textile machines rather than opposing their introduction altogether. Similarly, today's workers have not resisted the use of artificial intelligence and robotics in the workplace but want to see a rising level of family incomes, which have been stagnant for years.[19]

A scenario more promising than slowing down technological advance is channeling it so as to sustain productive employment of human beings. Technology can be put to good use by small businesses in rural areas as well as in cities. Decentralized production of agriculture already is seen as a good thing, and decentralized production of goods would also be a positive development because more people would be employed closer to markets.

Another technology-induced factor is less obvious but is potentially the most important impact of social media on society. James Madison, writing *Federalist Paper No. 10*, cautioned against a pure or direct democracy (such as the Internet now offers us) on grounds that it would lead to factionalism.[20] Indeed, the form of direct democracy that technology has made possible has led, in the United States and Europe, to extreme forms of factionalism, bordering in some instances on anarchy.[21] Practicing representative democracy has become more of a challenge because a form of direct democracy is undermining the institutions that have made representative democracy a vibrant reality in the United States.

The challenge to representative or parliamentary democracy is not an American phenomenon alone. It has its counterparts in Britain and in the European Union. In Russia and China, authoritarian governments, backed by strong nationalist instincts are, for now, holding in check the centrifugal effects of the new technology.

IMPLICATIONS FOR WORLD ORDER

David Brooks wrote in a column in *The New York Times* (July 1, 2016) that "in country after country the main battle lines of debate are evolving toward the open/closed framework."[22] He was referring to the tension between nationalism and globalization. Cast in American political terms, as Brooks did in his column, "open" refers to "open borders, free trade, cosmopolitan culture and global intervention." "Closed" refers to "closed borders, trade barriers, local and nationalistic culture, and an America First foreign policy."

Brooks argued that this debate foreshadows a realignment of political parties along open and closed lines. It is certainly correct to say that this issue is one of the most fundamental questions underlying the systemic changes in global affairs today. It figured importantly in the 2016 US presidential election, where many voters seem to have supported what Brooks called a "closed framework." It is probably the question on which elections in Europe will turn during the next few years.

How this issue is resolved has enormous implications for cooperative security and for the future of humanity. If extreme nationalism, or a series of closed systems, carries the day, it will be very difficult, probably impossible, to construct an international coalition of nations committed to creating the conditions for a world without nuclear weapons. The same would very likely be true for cooperative efforts to stop and roll back climate change and other threats to civilization.

Nuclear weapons appeal to nations that believe they have to go it alone in an uncertain world, feel menaced by the superior forces of a neighbor, or think prestige comes from having a nuclear weapons stockpile. Bilateral, regional, or joint enterprises among nations to create the conditions for a world without nuclear weapons would be almost unimaginable in a world where the vision of cooperative security had vanished.

To return to Hedley Bull's summary of the general theories of international relations, it is likely that nuclear weapons would be the inevitable result of a world vision that is Hobbesian, that is, a world that is seen as "all against all." That vision was on prominent display in the American presidential election of 2016 and in President Trump's inaugural address on January 20, 2017.

A conflict of civilizations, as Samuel Huntington speculated at the end of the Cold War, is an image that terrorist groups have conjured up, quite deliberately.[23] China's belligerent actions in the South China Sea also lend support to that vision of the future. Vladimir Putin's rejection of Western values and his quest for a Eurasian Community also supports the notion that, far from moving toward a global society, the world is heading toward a system of national conglomerates at war with each other. That vision might prevail, but other more optimistic inclusionary visions are possible if given strong support from national governments.

How likely is it that the Hobbesian view will dominate US and world politics? Megatrends in human affairs seem to be moving in the direction of more, rather than less, interdependence. Naturally, these trends affect different parts of the globe in different ways. Some nations may be able to exist indefinitely as a "garrison state," as Eisenhower put it. That does not appear to be the route to peace and prosperity. Global integration has benefited millions of people around the world. Clearly, its benefits will need to be more evenly divided among and within nations, but that should be a feasible project. A global open society, rather than a series of closed societies, is receiving powerful support from technology enterprises. Technological change is gradually penetrating almost every part of the world in ways that are likely to be irreversible. Technology may even succeed over time in reducing or eliminating some of globalization's economic advantages as labor costs become a smaller part of decisions about where to locate factories.

Nationalism will not cease to be a dynamic force on the international scene. It will remain so for decades because it offers a satisfying sense of belonging to a group with common history, culture, and values. This is why immigrants are seen as threatening. But nationalism need not become what it has been recently—inward looking and hostile to outside influences. There are costs in such attitudes, as Brexit reminds us. A narrowly conceived nationalism ultimately is antithetical to economic success, as well as to humanitarian values.

As this is written, the British pound has fallen sharply and the British government, despite its "Global Britain" slogan, has not found it easy to replace the market for British goods that the European Union offers. A 2016 report by the UK's Office for Budget Responsibility stated that potential growth will be 2.4 percentage points lower over the next five years and that $75 billion in additional borrowing can be attributed to Brexit. The pound's fall will add almost 2 percent to the level of consumer prices over the next two years.[24] Despite this warning to other nations, right-leaning, anti-EU populist parties in France, Germany, and the Netherlands, are presenting serious challenges to governing parties that support a stranger EU. Reportedly, Russian President Putin's own Russian political party has formed links with populist parties in Europe and is egging them on.[25]

EUROPE'S CRISIS

The implications of global change include many divisive issues, but the most politically potent of these wedge issues have occurred within the European Union:

- Mass migration into Europe from Africa and the Middle East;
- Popular resistance to the rules laid down by the European Union governing apparatus in Brussels;
- Perceived threats to national identities; and
- Disruptions in traditional economic activities.

Across Europe, right-wing nationalist parties have challenged the liberal internationalist consensus that prevailed for decades and have gained political support from dissatisfied electorates. The forces of history and culture are strong in Europe as elsewhere. Nationalism is a powerful tool and it is being used to mobilize populations within the nations of Europe. A sense of Europe as a homeland has caught on among the younger generation, but not among those who control the levers of power in some European governments, populations disadvantaged by the global and EU economies, or those disturbed by immigration from the Middle East and Africa. The Brexit vote clearly showed this. Elections in other EU nations will be a test of how widespread the rejection of the EU and the restoration of nationalism in Europe has become. The presidential election in France that concluded with the election of Emmanuel Macron in 2017 was a major victory for pro-EU forces.

Incremental integration based on economic enterprises has been the method Europeans have used since Jean Monnet and Robert Schuman proposed the European Coal and Steel Community in 1950. But an underlying problem in Europe is that integration had proceeded far enough to gain broad support for a common currency, but not far enough to create the political unity necessary to successfully operate one. In an age distinguished by a globalized economy, which promotes fragmentation in the labor market, and by the communications revolution, which fosters direct democracy but can undermine representative democracy, the "permanent revolution" that Putin referred to several years ago is at work today in Europe. New strategies and new modes of public discourse will have to be found if the European unity project is to be saved.

NORMS FOR THE EMERGING
INTERNATIONAL REGIME

Experience in the United States during the long election season in 2016 has raised questions about the impact of "fake news." For example, in Washington, DC, a man with an assault rifle entered a pizza restaurant filled with families to see for himself whether Hillary Clinton was running a ring there to exploit children for sexual purposes, as he had heard repeatedly from fake news stories on the Internet.[26] Laws against hate speech are more restrictive in Europe and Israel than in the United States, but recent experience may lead to a debate about speech laws in the United States.

Scholars Jennifer Allen and George Norris have written about limits on hate speech in various countries.[27] They pointed out that nations that had recent experience with hate speech and genocide, as in Europe, tended to be influenced by that experience in their approach to speech laws. They saw the United States as less influenced by that experience and thus enjoying freedom of speech and First Amendment laws that "represent an extreme on the spectrum of permitted violent speech." This is my condensed version of their assessment:

> The German Basic Law guarantees freedom of expression and dissemination of opinions but also allows limitations on this freedom. Article 1 declares that human dignity is the right of every citizen and that it must be protected.

Accordingly, the Penal Code criminalizes speech that is an assault on human dignity. No finding of intent to create harm is required.

Israel's Basic Law does not include the right to freedom of speech but the Israeli Supreme Court has upheld that right but has determined that limits are permissible based on a finding that a probable danger to public peace has been created. Human dignity is protected in the Basic Law on Human Dignity and Liberty; Israel has adopted laws that criminalize hate speech.

The European Union's Charter of Fundamental Rights contains the right to freedom of expression without interference by public authorities. That said, the European Union also asks member states to criminalize speech that incites violence or hatred against groups or a member of a group identified by such criteria as race or religion or nationality. Both German and EU legal practice essentially accepts that people are entitled to their own opinions, but not to their own facts, the denial of generally agreed facts, like the Holocaust, being seen as a form of hate speech, subject to limits.

The United States Constitution states that Congress shall make no law abridging the freedom of speech. Only speech that incites immediate violent action has become subject to criminalization. Human dignity appears to be less important than the right of free speech. Obviously, US law is not absolutist in terms of allowing hate speech but the latitude for regulating this kind of speech is much more restricted than is the case in Europe and Israel.

Sooner or later, the US Supreme Court will probably consider whether Internet speech that leads to violence by being repeated many times as fact over the Internet should be criminalized. Self-regulation by websites might be preferable, but it is hard to see how this can come about as a practical solution except as part of a general set of norms and rules that are voluntarily accepted by millions of Internet users.[28]

Americans already have begun to inquire about the adequacy of Internet servers' rules regarding fake news. Probably questions will arise regarding freedom of access to the Web, freedom of association via the Web, and freedom of those associations to act in keeping with their own values. Concerns are being voiced about Russia's use of "trolls" which, in effect, are online agents of influence. It is possible that the impulse to limit the freedoms offered by the Web will cause pressures that would be unnecessarily restrictive, representing a major test for all democracies. This was the view expressed in a March 2017 vote by the US Senate.[29] And the Supreme Court, as this is written, has before it a case involving a person in North Carolina who in accord with a North Carolina law, was denied the right to view certain websites.[30]

Scientists have created standards for exploitation of new scientific developments like genetic modifications and these have been fairly successful in guiding research and applications.[31] Likewise, citizens of democracies have the ability and the responsibility to push back against technology when it is perceived to work against their welfare. Implicit rules of behavior regarding the Web seem to be emerging in Western democracies, although there is still, quite naturally, much debate about them, particularly about privacy and about misuse of the Web for fake news and other mischief. The following set of rules is offered as a hypothetical example:

1. Freedom of access to information available on the Internet;
2. Freedom of association via the Internet both domestically and across frontiers;
3. Freedom to act, as associations, in accordance with national norms and laws and, increasingly, in accordance with globally accepted standards of human rights;
4. Freedom of people to adapt to the intrusion of new ideas and to cultural change or to opt out if they willingly and wittingly desire to do so;
5. The inherent right to privacy of citizens in their communications via the Internet; and
6. The willingness of governments to compromise with major technology enterprises where this would not jeopardize the safety and security of their citizens.

These hypothetical rules are oriented toward individual citizens because it is their collective behavior in their use of the Internet that has suggested how citizens in democracies think about the ways they want to communicate with each other. The rules are not necessarily beneficial in terms of the ability of organized society, typically governments, to mobilize their citizens in support of cooperative security negotiations and agreements because existential threats to humanity's very existence require cooperation among nations, which may appear occasionally to be at odds with national interests.

So long as national governments hold the responsibility for negotiating and implementing cooperative security agreements, they will need to act coherently and in a sustained manner in their interactions with other governments, and this may demand some modifications in the rules. For example, the Islamic State in Iraq and Syria (ISIS) has utilized the Internet as an effective recruiting tool. "Lone wolf" attacks on Americans in San Bernardino, California, and Orlando, Florida, evidently were inspired by ISIS propaganda disseminated over the Internet. Instructions may be transmitted to would-be terrorists via the Internet. American recruits for

ISIS forces in the Middle East were motivated to travel to Syria after hearing ISIS harangues on the Web. One of the most effective speakers for the ISIS cause was an American imam, Anwar al-Awlaki, killed in Yemen in an American drone attack. ISIS messaging also contains practical advice on bomb-making. Beheadings have been used to spread terror via the Internet.

Should Internet servers impose stricter rules regarding the use of the Internet? Already in place in Russia and China, modest rule changes regarding the use of the Internet also have been gradually put in place in the United States in response to abuses.[32] Governments at all levels and technology companies deserve credit for acting to prevent gross misuse of the Internet, but restricting free speech and access to information has to be managed with extreme care.

It would not be right to infer that social media currently are in the driver's seat in influencing public opinion, but it does seem fair to say that at this stage in the development of a new social order, democratic representative government is under pressure from a technology that tends to favor participatory democracy while weakening the institutions of representative governance. Russia and China have responded to this situation by marshalling the tools of authoritarian governance to restrict access of their citizens to Internet information or to overwhelm external sources of information with guidance generated by pro-government internal sources of information. In doing this, they may be paying a price in terms of reduced competitiveness in the economic and cultural spheres but, so far, the price has not deterred them from continuing the practice. The United States, which led the way into the digital age, has mostly accepted the norms listed above, but with some reluctance and misgivings in a number of well-publicized cases.

In June 2016, a federal court ruled that Internet companies can be treated as utilities and regulated as such by governments.[33] This ruling has been challenged by the US Senate, among others, and is likely to be an issue for the US legal system for years to come. The US government has also insisted on having access to encrypted material when national interests seem to require it. This has been strongly resisted by major technology enterprises such as Google, Apple, and Microsoft.[34] These companies argue that enabling governments to have access to private citizens' encrypted messages is contrary to the principle of guaranteed privacy, which is one of their main selling points.

A COURSE CORRECTION FOR GLOBALIZATION

President Obama's final address to the UN General Assembly on September 20, 2016, focused at length on globalization and international trade, and their domestic impact. "We all face a choice," he said. "We can choose to press forward with a better model of cooperation and integration, or we can retreat into a world sharply divided, and ultimately in conflict, along age-old lines of nation and tribe and race and religion."[35]

The president said that "we cannot unwind integration any more than we can stuff technology back into a box," but he called for a "course correction." He identified four challenges to global integration, which are paraphrased as follows:

- Globalization and rapid progress in technology have contributed to widening the gap between rich and poor, both within and between nations;
- Governance has not kept up with the massive changes in a world that requires open societies in order to prosper, and also protection of sensitive information associated with ever-more-powerful technologies since these technologies can be used for destructive purposes, as well as constructive ones;
- Traditional national and local identities are seen as incompatible with global integration, and the resulting collision of cultures leads to an impulse to dehumanize or dominate other groups; and
- International cooperation requires the contentious act of giving up some freedom of action and the complex task of building up international capacity to deal with the existential challenges of the twenty-first century, one of which is nuclear war.

President Obama hinted at one of the intangible assets of a global society when he said that young people appeared to be "more empathetic and compassionate towards their fellow human beings than previous generations." He attributed this in part to "young people's access to information about other peoples and places—an understanding that is unique in human history that their future is bound with the fates of other human beings on the other side of the world." The president added that young Americans are "unencumbered by what is, but are instead ready to seize what ought to be."[36]

Writing in the May/June 2016 issue of *Foreign Affairs*, Kishore Mahbubani and Lawrence Summers argued that "despite the daily headlines that scream doom and gloom, the world is actually coming together, not falling apart . . . driven primarily by the injection of Western DNA into other civilizations."[37] That description underestimated the resistance of ancient civilizations to changing their ways but it was right to suggest that globalization is an essentially Western idea. It has succeeded not just because of the economic advantages it confers, but also because it has substantially raised the living standards of people all over the world, and because it offers the vision of an open society.

The authors of this article warned that this trend could be reversed or slowed: "It would be a terrible shame if the West walked away from the very international order that it created after World War II."[38] And one of the authors, Lawrence Summers, subsequently wrote a short article for *The Washington Post* arguing for "responsible nationalism" that recognized the powerful influence of unbridled nationalism and pointed to "the vastly better performance of the global system after World War II" than between World War I and World War II.[39]

The economic benefits of a globalized economy are not likely to be so overwhelming that they will lead to a fusion of civilizations and a global society, or even sustain support for the changes inherent in an integrated global economy. Active leadership by major nations, like the United States, will be needed to create the conditions that make global economic integration work for nations and their peoples. Difficult domestic reforms will be required to provide for a more equitable distribution of the wealth generated by globalization and technology and to look after the people whose lives are disrupted by these forces. This was the main lesson of events in the United States and Europe in 2016.

SUMMING UP

The fundamentals of the international system have been changing rapidly and that process will continue, often in unpredictable ways.[40] National governments are still the main engines of decision making in most, if not all, global and regional affairs, and are likely to remain so for decades. Theirs will be the chief responsibility for championing cooperative security agreements to spare the world from destruction, whether by nuclear holocaust, disease, or the effects of climate change. National governments will have new tools made possible by the forces of technology and global integration. They could harness these tools to promote a rational and informed public conversation that would lead to policies which might prevent the quite foreseeable disasters that otherwise lie ahead. Will the forces of nationalism work against that? They could, but a citizenry armed with the facts should be a bulwark against them. If not, their failure will be a failure for all humanity.

When large numbers of people feel that globalization is hurting them, they will rebel. Is there a connection between policies to tame globalization, or make it more responsible, and policies to roll back existential threats to all of humanity? Of course there is. Governments cannot on the one hand face a populace made miserable by economic and cultural dislocations, and on the other hand ask them to support sweeping agreements with other nations and to delegate some of their own nation's sovereignty to international institutions. There is some scholarly evidence for these propositions, too. A 1994 study by Etel Solingen concluded that there was "impressive empirical evidence" to support the proposition that coalition governments pursuing economic liberalization are more likely to embrace regional nuclear regimes than are inward-looking, nationalist, and radical coalitions.[41]

Andrei Sakharov, the Russian physicist and human rights activist, had an uncanny ability to analyze human events and to prophesy their future course. Observing the enormous changes that were taking place in his lifetime, he concluded that chaos was likely to persist for many decades. His reaction to that prophecy offered the germ of a strategy that should guide us today. Governments, he said, should work to overcome divisions among peoples and, at a minimum, avoid actions that encourage hostilities among them.[42] Following that general idea requires (1) some institutionalized way of promoting cooperative security, and (2) a shared objective that is bold enough to attract support but practical enough to be seen as achievable.

The proper management of global change is a complicated business and clearly has not been mastered in any advanced nation. There is reason to believe, based on experience with other existential issues like climate change, that major elements of public opinion can be rallied around causes that affect all of humanity, not just the interests of single nations. These causes, which have bilateral, regional, and global implications, will be examined in following chapters.

NOTES

1. James E. Goodby, "The Putin Doctrine and Preventive Diplomacy," *Foreign Service Journal*, November 2014.

2. Hans Kristensen and Robert Norris, "Status of World Nuclear Forces," *Federation of American Scientists*, https://fas.org/issues/nuclear-weapons/status-world-nuclear-forces/.

3. Arnau Busquets Guàrdia, "How Brexit Vote Broke Down," *Politico* (June 24–25, 2016), http://www.politico.eu/article/graphics-how-the-uk-voted-eu-referendum-brexit-demographics-age-education-party-london-final-results/.

4. Thomas B. Edsall, "The Great Democratic Inversion," *The New York Times* (October 27, 2016).

5. One particularly relevant example comes from Dietrich Jung, "Globalization, State Formation, and Religion in the Middle East: Is Islam Incompatible with Democracy?" *Taylor&Francis Online* (March 4, 2011), http://www.tandfonline.com/doi/abs/10.1080/1600910X.2004.9672877?journalCode=rdis20. This article identifies tensions between the Middle East and globalization, particularly with regard to the rise of political Islam "as the embodiment of cultural particularism in the ongoing globalization process," which is seen as an imposition of Western

theories and norms. Globalization is seen as a foreign imposition throughout much of the Middle East.

6. Hedley Bull, *The Anarchical Society: A Study of Order in World Politics* (New York: Columbia University Press, 1977).

7. Ibid.

8. Ibid.

9. Ibid.

10. John Markoff, "Tech Giants Gather to Devise Real Ethics for Artificial Intelligence," *The New York Times* (September 2, 2016).

11. Richard Haass speaks of nonsovereign groups like NGOs and Silicon Valley corporations and says "room must be found for the meaningful participation of relevant nonsovereign entities in an order predicated on sovereign obligation," in chapter 10, "World Order 2.0," *A World in Disarray: American Foreign Policy and the Crisis of the Old Order* (New York: Penguin Press, 2017), 255.

12. Farhad Manjoo, "Social Media's Globe-Shaking Power," *The New York Times* (November 16, 2016), https://www.nytimes.com/2016/11/17/technology/social-medias-globe-shaking-power.html.

13. Marissa Lang, "2016 Presidential Election Circus: Is Social Media the Cause?" *San Francisco Chronicle* (April 5, 2016), http://www.govtech.com/social/2016-Presidential-Election-Circus-Is-Social-Media-the-Cause.html.

14. Matt Kapko, "How Social Media Is Shaping the 2016 Presidential Election," *CIO* (September 29, 2016), http://www.cio.com/article/3125120/social-networking/how-social-media-is-shaping-the-2016-presidential-election.html.

15. Eric Lipton, David E. Sanger, and Scott Shane, "The Perfect Weapon: How Russian Cyberpower Invaded the US," *The New York Times* (December 13, 2016).

16. Mike Isaac, "Facebook Said to Create Censorship Tool to Get Back into China," *The New York Times* (November 22, 2016).

17. Steve Lohr, "Robots Will Take Jobs, but Not as Fast as Some Fear, New Report Says," *The New York Times* (January 12, 2017).

18. Alvin Toffler, *Future Shock* (New York: Random House, 1970).

19. Paul Krugman, "Sympathy for the Luddites," *The New York Times* (June 14, 2013). Like many other analysts, Krugman proposed a guaranteed minimum income financed by taxes on profits and/or investment income.

20. James Madison, https://www.congress.gov/resources/display/content/The+Federalist+Papers#TheFederalistPapers-10.

21. Derek Hawking, "'Black Bloc' Protests Return for Trump Era, Leaving Flames, Broken Windows from D.C. to Berkeley," *The Washington Post* (February 2, 2017).

22. David Brooks, "The Coming Political Realignment," *The New York Times* (July 1, 2016).

23. Samuel P. Huntington, *The Clash of Civilizations and the Remaking of World Order* (New York: Simon & Schuster, 1996).

24. Stephen Castle, "With Philip Hammond's Plan, UK Shelves Austerity," *The New York Times* (November 23, 2016).

25. Peter Foster and Matthew Holehouse, "Russia Accused of Clandestine Funding of European Parties as US Conducts Major Review of Vladimir Putin's Strategy," *The Telegraph* (January 16, 2016).

26. Faiz Siddiqui and Susan Svrluga, "N.C. Man Told Police He Went to D.C. Pizzeria with Gun to Investigate Conspiracy Theory," *The Washington Post* (December 5, 2016), https://www.washingtonpost.com/news/local/wp/2016/12/04/d-c-police-respond-to-report-of-a-man-with-a-gun-at-comet-ping-pong-restaurant/?utm_term=.d7807f6974b4.

27. Jennifer M. Allen and George H. Norris, "Is Genocide Different? Dealing with Hate Speech in Post-Genocide Society," *Journal of International Law & International Relations* 146 (Fall 2011).

28. Timothy Garton Ash has written about the free speech issue in *Free Speech: Ten Principles for a Connected World*. New Haven, CT: Yale University Press, 2016.

29. Cecilia Kang, "Congress Moves to Strike Internet Privacy Rules from Obama Era," *The New York Times* (March 23, 2017), https://www.nytimes.com/2017/03/23/technology/congress-moves-to-strike-internet-privacy-rules-from-obama-era.html?_r=0.

30. Steven Nelson, "Supreme Court Reviews Felony for Accessing Facebook," *U.S. News and World Report* (February 24, 2017).

31. Paul Berg, "Meetings That Changed the World: Asilomar 1975: DNA Modification Secured," *Nature* 455 (September 18, 2008): 290–91. See also Asilomar guidelines on recombinant DNA.

32. See, for example, on facebook.com, "Controversial, Harmful and Hateful Speech on Facebook," signed by Marne Levine, VP of Global Public Policy, May 28, 2013.

33. Cecilia Kang, "Court Backs Rules Treating Internet as Utility, Not Luxury," *The New York Times* (June 14, 2016), https://www.nytimes.com/2016/06/15/technology/net-neutrality-fcc-appeals-court-ruling.html.

34. An example was the FBI request in connection with the San Bernardino shooting. Matt Zapotosky, "FBI Has Accessed San Bernardino Shooter's Phone Without Apple's Help," *Washington Post* (March 28, 2016), https://www.washingtonpost.com/world/national-security/fbi-has-accessed-san-bernardino-shooters-phone-without-apples-help/2016/03/28/e593a0e2-f52b-11e5-9804-537defcc3cf6_story.html?utm_term=.44af839b9cf8.

35. President Barack Obama, "Address by President Obama to the 71st Session of the United Nations General Assembly," September 20, 2016.

36. Ibid.

37. Kishore Mahbubani and Lawrence H. Summers, "The Fusion of Civilizations: The Case for Global Optimism," *Foreign Affairs* (May/June 2016).

38. Ibid.

39. Lawrence Summers, "How to Embrace Nationalism Responsibly," *The Washington Post* (July 10, 2016).

40. For an excellent analysis of the challenges the international system is facing and how it is responding, see Richard Haass, *A World in Disarray*, 2017.

41. Etel Solingen, "The Political Enemy of Nuclear Restraint," *International Security* 19 (Fall 1994).

42. Sidney Drell and George Shultz, eds., *Andrei Sakharov: The Conscience of Humanity* (Stanford, CA: Hoover Institution Press, 2015).

Four

The Potential for Regional Cooperative Security Negotiations

> Competition has been shown to be useful up to a certain point and no further, but cooperation, which is the thing we must strive for today, begins where competition leaves off.
>
> —Franklin Delano Roosevelt

If regional conflicts are potentially metastable and an unpredictable tipping point lurks just over the horizon, the following questions need to be examined:

- What is the impact of nuclear weapons on regional conflicts?
- Do they forestall escalation?
- Do they help resolve disputes?
- Can regional organizations help achieve security and cooperation?
- Are there synergies between global and regional cooperative security arrangements that could yield mutually beneficial results?

DO NUCLEAR WEAPONS HELP ACHIEVE REGIONAL PEACE SETTLEMENTS?

Nuclear weapons are frequently depicted as benign instruments of peace. During the Cold War's nuclear arms race between the United States and the Soviet Union, a large sign outside the USAF Strategic Air Command Headquarters in Omaha, Nebraska, proclaimed, "Peace Is Our Profession." The rationale was that the presence of nuclear weapons and the ability to deliver them on target deters armed conflict. The long peace between major powers since 1945 supported that conclusion and still does. But can a cause-and-effect correlation be established between the presence of nuclear weapons and the peaceful conditions they purportedly have engendered?[1] That is difficult to prove.

65

Each of the conflicts in Northeast Asia, South Asia, and the Middle East obviously stems from a long-standing intractable dispute. It is far from clear that the main effect of nuclear weapons has been to prevent these disputes from boiling over into open warfare. It can be argued instead that these weapons turned disputes that might have been resolved into protracted "frozen conflicts" and made cooperative security in these regions almost impossible. The potential for nuclear war exists any time two hostile nations armed with nuclear weapons confront each other, and so passing from competition to cooperation between such countries should be a top priority. We should try to move from a metastable condition to a stable condition.

If nuclear weapons are perceived to be instruments of peace, the tendency in conflict zones will be to leave things as they are: no war, no peace, and very little cooperation. This perpetuates a dangerous situation. The impact of nuclear weapons in the Middle East, South Asia, and Northeast Asia, as I see it, will be discussed in the following pages.

NORTHEAST ASIA

In Northeast Asia, the case is strong that the presence of nuclear weapons in Korea turned a bitter relationship between North and South into a struggle that now threatens to engulf all of Northeast Asia and beyond. Here is the story.

North Korea's first president, Kim Il Sung, became convinced that the nation he founded was entitled to have nuclear weapons, particularly because his perceived enemy, the United States, had threatened their use during the 1950–1953 Korean War and had deployed short-range nuclear weapons in South Korea after the war. He initiated an indigenous nuclear power program in the 1950s with the support of his ally, the Soviet Union, probably planning to transition to a weapons program in due course, if circumstances warranted that. This is the route followed by other possessors of nuclear weapons. These programs create a "breakout potential" that allows a nation to build the infrastructure and technical expertise necessary to build a nuclear bomb.

When the Soviet Union collapsed in 1991, it is probable that Kim Il Sung became convinced that nuclear weapons were a matter of regime survival. The 1991 decision by President George H. W. Bush to withdraw American nuclear weapons that had been deployed with American troops in South Korea may have persuaded President Kim Il Sung that he had other options, or he may have decided just to buy time. In any event, he entered into agreements with the South Korean government in 1991–1992 that renounced nuclear weapons and established a charter for closer

North-South relations, the so-called Basic Agreement.[2] These agreements failed to bring about a rapprochement in Korea and with the United States. In fact, relations between the North and South deteriorated badly. A 5-megawatt reactor was defueled without accounting for the plutonium that could be used in a nuclear weapon. By early 1994, there was talk in Washington of bombing North Korea's nuclear facilities.[3]

Defying the Clinton administration's wishes, former President Carter undertook a mission to Pyongyang in June 1994 and reached an understanding with Kim Il Sung. The North Korean leader agreed to discuss a freeze on his nuclear program with the United States. Fate intervened soon thereafter: Kim Il Sung died suddenly on July 8, 1994. His son, Kim Jong Il, took his place and honored his father's offer. The result was the negotiation of a US–DPRK Agreed Framework, which offered North Korea assistance in civil nuclear power programs (light water reactors) and an improvement in relations with the United States in return for closing down its plutonium production facilities.[4] An important part of the agreement was the creation of an implementing organization based in New York, the Korean Peninsula Energy Development Organization (KEDO).

In the last years of the Clinton administration, former Secretary of Defense William J. Perry was appointed to explore the possibilities for agreements with North Korea that would definitively end the nation's missile and nuclear-weapons programs.[5] This process became known as the Perry Process and it yielded progress sufficient to justify a visit to the North Korean capital, Pyongyang, by Secretary of State Madeleine Albright and a visit to Washington by North Korean special envoy Jo Myong Rok. Albright's successor as secretary of state, General Colin Powell, expected to build on Perry's achievements but he was overruled by President George W. Bush in March 2001, the president opting for his own review of policy.

That decision turned out to be a serious blow to hopes for an end to North Korea's nuclear programs. The momentum imparted to US-DPRK negotiations by the withdrawal of US nuclear weapons from Korea in 1991 and the Agreed Framework of 1994 evaporated over the first years of the Bush administration. North Korean noncompliance with the Agreed Framework was discovered when in 2002 evidence of a clandestine uranium-enrichment facility in North Korea came to light. Relations again deteriorated between Pyongyang, Seoul, and Washington.

Hopes for rebuilding momentum toward a peace settlement were raised when Six-Party Talks were inaugurated in 2003. These included China, Japan, Russia, the United States, and North and South Korea. For a while these talks showed signs of progress, including an agreement on a nuclear-weapon-free Korean Peninsula. But verification and North

Korean missile flight testing proved to be more than the parties could handle. The talks deteriorated and ended in 2009.[6]

The Obama administration took office in 2009 with the expressed hope of inaugurating an era of negotiation. President Obama said in a speech in Cairo on June 4, 2009, that "Whatever we think of the past, we must not be prisoners of it. Our problems must be dealt with through partnership; progress must be shared."[7]

Kim Jong Il died in 2011 and was succeeded by his son, Kim Jong Un, a man who rapidly established his power position with purges and executions of senior military and civilian officials, also including his uncle and later his half-brother. There was one semisuccess with North Korea, a US-DPRK understanding on February 29, 2012. It became known as the Leap Day Agreement and provided for a moratorium on DPRK nuclear test explosions and ballistic missile tests.[8] This promising beginning ended abruptly when North Korea insisted that the agreement allowed for satellite launches and proceeded to launch a satellite with a ballistic missile in April 2012. The Obama administration was convinced that ballistic missiles used for satellite launches amounted to a flight test of ballistic missiles that could be used to deliver nuclear warheads, and so the agreement was abruptly terminated.

After that, the Obama administration adopted a policy of "strategic patience," essentially a way of disengaging. There were no more negotiations regarding North Korea's nuclear-weapons program during the Obama administration. By the summer of 2016, North Korea had conducted five nuclear test explosions.[9] In his 2017 New Year's address to the nation, Kim Jong Un said that North Korea was entering a stage of preparations for a long-range ballistic missile launch.[10]

Politically, the status as of early 2017 is that Kim Jong Un seems to have consolidated his hold on power. He and previous North Korean leaders (his father and grandfather) have all stated their willingness to negotiate with the United States and other nations in the region, and on occasion progress has been made toward a settlement. But North Korea has a nuclear-weapons program that has already generated a significant nuclear arsenal of possibly twenty warheads, and its ballistic missile program made substantial advances in 2016.[11] North Korea's constitution has been amended to state that North Korea is a nuclear-weapon state and the DPRK government has declined to repeat earlier statements about a nuclear-weapon-free Korean Peninsula. In contrast to Great Britain, China, France, Russia, and the United States, North Korea did vote in 2016 in favor of a General Assembly Resolution asking for negotiations on a treaty to ban nuclear weapons but did not show up when talks first got underway in March 2017.[12] Unlike other possessors of nuclear weapons, North Korea has not declared a moratorium on explosive nuclear tests.

Assessment

Does this history show that US nuclear weapons in South Korea prevented armed conflict on the Korean Peninsula? Does it show that removal of US nuclear weapons based in South Korea encouraged conflict? Or does it perhaps show that nuclear weapons exacerbated the dispute between North and South Korea and between North Korea and the United States? What does it say, in short, about the impact of nuclear weapons on achieving a peaceful settlement of issues that have made Northeast Asia one of the world's centers of dangerous tensions? Some things are clear:

- Nuclear weapons have not deterred military actions that both sides find repugnant, whether they be military actions by North Korea against South Korean military assets or annual large-scale joint military exercises by American and South Korean forces.
- Evidence that nuclear weapons deterred full-scale war between North Korea and South Korea and its ally, the United States, is available only in the sense that such a war never happened after 1953. But South Korea has built a powerful conventional deterrent, making it very unlikely that a North Korean invasion could achieve any reasonable objective. North Korea has artillery within range of Seoul, the South Korean capital, and could devastate the city before a counterattack by the South eliminated that capacity. This condition is called deterrence by denial, which appears suitable to South Korea's circumstances, and perhaps to those of North Korea.
- Negotiations focused mainly on nuclear weapons have not succeeded and may have raised tensions.

A case can be made that the chances of reaching a potential settlement in Korea would have been better if nuclear weapons had never entered the equation, or if the openings in 1992 and 1994 had been pursued more vigorously.

SOUTH ASIA

South Asia offers a different set of lessons about the impact of nuclear weapons on regional peace and stability, based on the experience of two sovereign nations that fought three limited wars against each other. One of them, India, possessed greater conventional military strength than the other, Pakistan, a situation that might have encouraged Pakistan to acquire nuclear weapons first. That did not happen. Instead, India diverted plutonium from a reactor that Canada had provided to help meet India's electrical power needs. In 1974, India tested a nuclear device that it called an experiment in using nuclear explosions for peaceful purposes.[13] That was not followed by Pakistani nuclear test explosions. But it did encourage A. Q. Kahn, a Pakistani engineer working for URENCO in the Netherlands, to steal the plans for a uranium enrichment facility based on gas centrifuges.[14] In 1998, an Indian government run by the Hindu nationalist party decided that India's status as a great power required that it have nuclear weapons. The rationale was not based so much on a military threat from Pakistan as on rivalry with China. China by that time was a recognized nuclear-weapon state under the Non-Proliferation Treaty, while India was not.

India had built the infrastructure for a nuclear-weapons program by 1998, including separating plutonium from reactors that it had refused to place under international safeguards. It was not under any legal obligation to do so, having declined to become a signatory of the Non-Proliferation Treaty (NPT), which both India and Pakistan regarded as discriminatory.

On May 11–13, 1998, India conducted five nuclear test explosions. This time Pakistan followed suit with five test explosions on May 28, 1998. A. Q. Khan, using the stolen blueprints for a uranium enrichment plant, oversaw the construction of a uranium enrichment facility at Ras Koh Hills in Pakistan. Pakistan built the infrastructure for a nuclear-weapons program also with help from China, which provided information regarding nuclear warhead design.[15] Since then, Pakistan has built plutonium production facilities and now incorporates plutonium in its nuclear-weapons program.[16] Both India and Pakistan have built delivery systems capable of reaching each other's territory and beyond.

Did the acquisition of significant nuclear arsenals by both nations by the early twenty-first century make war between them less likely? Most experts believe that Pakistan has tended to misjudge the effects of nuclear deterrence on India, leading to attacks on India that might not have happened in the pre-nuclear age.[17] The first of these attacks took place in 1999 at Kargil, Jammu and Kashmir. The conflict seems to have been based on a calculation by General Pervez Musharraf, then in control of the government of Pakistan, that India would be deterred from responding to the Pakistani military actions. That calculation was wrong. India did respond with a counterattack that repulsed Pakistani forces and reinstated the status quo. Two other seemingly Pakistani-inspired attacks on India were mounted by terrorist forces. The first, an armed attack on India's parliament building in New Delhi, took place on December 13, 2001. The second, in Mumbai on November 26–29, 2008, was a terrorist attack on civilians aimed at inflicting as many casualties as possible.[18] The reasons for the attacks are obscure but likely related to Pakistan's hopes to establish what it called "strategic depth" in Afghanistan. The calculation probably was that terror attacks would not be considered a casus belli, an assumption that was correct in these two cases but may not always be so.

Even though India did not respond with an attack on Pakistan in either event, the rising tensions between the two nations led to military decisions on both sides that could have disastrous consequences in a future crisis. One such crisis occurred in September 2016 when a Pakistani terror attack on Indian military posts in Kashmir killed several Indian soldiers and led to an Indian military incursion across the Line of Control.[19] Probing for where the threshold of nuclear response may be is a dangerous game.

The Indian military has adopted a strategy it calls Cold Start.[20] That strategy theoretically gives the Indian armed forces the capability of launching a major ground attack on Pakistan without any mobilization. Pakistani leaders are understandably concerned about this strategy. To them, it amounts to India gearing up its conventional superiority to launch a surprise attack. Their answer has been to develop their capabilities in so-called tactical nuclear weaponry. Small and portable, these nuclear weapons could be launched with short-range missile systems. They also are vulnerable to seizure by terrorist groups. Now there is discussion in India about developing an Indian counterpart to Pakistan's tactical nuclear capabilities.[21]

The Pakistani capability in short-range nuclear forces was further refined after the American attack in February 2012 on the compound in Abbottabad where Osama bin Laden was living. Presumably seeing this as an illustration of the type of attack the United States' military was capable of mounting, Pakistani commanders began to worry that the same kind of attack might be used to seize their nuclear weapons. Their solution to this perceived problem was to deploy mobile tactical systems with already mated nuclear warheads so that nuclear weapons would not be stored in fixed and known locations.

Currently, Pakistan is rapidly building up its nuclear arsenal, based both on plutonium and uranium, on missiles and on aircraft. India, in the meantime, has a fast-growing economy that now is much larger than Pakistan's. The two countries obviously would benefit from increased economic cooperation, and there has been improvement in that area. But the action-reaction cycle in their military relationship continues to be a drag on their ability to engage in cooperative security efforts, to their mutual loss.

Assessment

What effect have nuclear weapons had in South Asia on preventing war and encouraging a political settlement? It appears to have been mostly negative. The scope of actions that a nuclear deterrent could prevent has been dangerously miscalculated, especially by Pakistan. India has made decisions that have encouraged Pakistan to rely more on nuclear weapons that are vulnerable to terrorist seizure. The main hope for escaping from this deterrence trap can be found in developing economic cooperation, but that may take more time than may be available to prevent a nuclear disaster.

Confidence-building measures and agreements that would restrain the arms race in the subcontinent, especially one that caused India to refrain from building a tactical nuclear force, probably could be devised. But unless and until China accepts limitations on its own nuclear forces, the China-India competition will feed into Pakistan's competition with India, making cooperative security almost impossible to achieve. This, of course, is a negative example of the synergy between global and regional rivalries, because China is influenced by what Russia and the United States do.

THE MIDDLE EAST

The Middle East is the most complex and now perhaps the most unstable of the regional dispute zones. Israel has never acknowledged that it possesses nuclear weapons, but it is widely believed to possess a stockpile of perhaps two hundred of them. Iraq had a civil nuclear program under Saddam Hussein that was generally seen as the precursor to building a plutonium-based breakout potential. Saddam's Osirak reactor was destroyed by Israel in a bombing attack in 1981. Refusing to abandon the nuclear option, Saddam proceeded to develop research on another approach, based on enriching uranium. This program was destroyed in the 1991 Gulf War, and a UN team later confirmed that all of Saddam's programs to produce weapons of mass destruction had been discovered and eliminated.

Nonetheless, in 2003, President George W. Bush ordered an invasion of Iraq, justifying the action on the grounds that Saddam still had a program to produce weapons of mass destruction (WMDs), biological and chemical, perhaps, as well as nuclear.[22] Neither pre- nor post-invasion searches led to the discovery of any evidence in Iraq of an infrastructure required to build such weapons and inspectors certified that Saddam had not had any such programs in 2003 when the invasion began.[23]

Iran became the next nation of concern. In 2003, the International Atomic Energy Agency (IAEA) reported that Iran had engaged in a number of nuclear activities contrary to its obligations under its Safeguards Agreement with the IAEA, which it had accepted as a party to the Non-Proliferation Treaty.[24] The IAEA also reported a number of concerns with respect to a possible military dimension to Iran's nuclear activities. The IAEA and then the UN Security Council called on Iran to suspend its enrichment and reprocessing activities while negotiations proceeded on a diplomatic solution. An agreement reached in October 2003 between Iran and France, Germany, and the United Kingdom, acting for the EU, led to a suspension of Iran's uranium enrichment, but this suspension effectively ended in 2005. The UN Security Council, the United States, the European Union, and others imposed increasingly stringent sanctions on Iran to encourage a negotiated outcome. In 2015, agreement was reached between Iran, the United States, Russia, China, the United Kingdom, France, and Germany on a substantial cutback in Iran's nuclear program, measures to ensure that remaining nuclear activities are exclusively peaceful, and a phased lifting of sanctions.[25] This agreement was entitled the Joint Comprehensive Plan of Action (JCPOA).

This result was opposed by Israel and other Middle Eastern states— Saudi Arabia in particular—who saw it as giving Iran a license to build an infrastructure that, over time, would allow it to break out of the agreement and mount a crash program to build nuclear weapons. Saudi Arabia has asserted that it will build a nuclear infrastructure to match Iran's.[26]

Syria briefly entered this history of preemption in 2007 when, in the early hours of September 6, Israeli aircraft attacked and destroyed a nuclear reactor being built at Al Kibar, Syria, with the help of North Korea. Neither Israel nor President Bashar al-Assad of Syria ever acknowledged that the attack had taken place.[27]

Assessment

How, then, have nuclear weapons influenced the prospect for peace and security in the Middle East? First, it is obvious that they have not deterred the kinds of conflicts that break out fairly frequently between Israel and organizations like Hamas in Gaza and Hezbollah in Lebanon. They did not deter Saddam's missile attacks on Israel during the first Persian Gulf War in 1991 nor the sporadic firing of missiles against Israel from Gaza since 2001. Their effect on preventing terrorism has been negligible and probably encouraged it as a method of asymmetric warfare.

A strategy on the part of Israel, generally supported by the United States, of not allowing any other Middle Eastern state to acquire a nuclear infrastructure suitable for achieving a breakout potential has generated

Israeli military action against Iraq and Syria and threatened military action against Iran.[28] But Israel has not been attacked with nuclear weapons because its neighbors do not have them, and that perhaps can be credited to Israel's preemption policy.

Backed by Egypt and other Arab states, a nuclear-free zone has been much discussed. Extensive consultations were carried out by a UN "facilitator," Jaakko Laajava of Finland, in 2011 and 2012, but no agreement has ever been reached. Israel's conventional forces so far have been able to cope with the threats to Israel, whereas just one thermonuclear explosion could pose an existential threat to the survival of the state. If a nuclear-free-zone agreement were adequately verified and enforced, Israel's security would be dramatically enhanced. Deterrence by denial would then be Israel's strategy, which, to a large degree, corresponds to its present situation.

CAN REGIONAL ORGANIZATIONS CONTRIBUTE TO PEACE AND SECURITY?

Regional organizations for broader cooperation in security affairs do not exist in Northeast Asia or in the Middle East. South Asia probably could rely on bilateral India-Pakistan cooperation. Europe's experience with the Conference on Security and Co-operation in Europe (CSCE), now the Organization for Security and Co-operation in Europe (OSCE), offers some relevant lessons. Experience in Europe, of course, cannot be translated automatically into precedents for other parts of the world, but the CSCE offers a superlative case study in how regional-global interactions can change the course of history.

One common denominator for all of the regions is the creation of a forum for negotiations. Otherwise, issues in various regions are different, or at least differently perceived, and the agenda for each region would have to be customized. A European forum was created through the mechanism of a thirty-five-party conference charged with making recommendations for improving security and cooperation in Europe. The diplomacy of that effort is worth a detailed examination because it shows that conditions do not have to be ideal in order to make significant progress. It also shows that transformational diplomacy is worth a try, even if the status quo seems easier to manage. In the next pages, I present a detailed narrative about the origins of the 1975 Helsinki Final Act as a case study of the creation of a regional organization for security and cooperation.[29]

A CASE STUDY OF CREATING A REGIONAL
ORGANIZATION FOR SECURITY AND COOPERATION

In August 1968, the combined armies of the Warsaw Pact invaded fellow Warsaw Pact member Czechoslovakia to suppress modest experiments with liberalization that the Prague government had initiated. The assessment of Western governments, including the US government, following that event was that, at a minimum, the strategic objective of the Soviet Union was to consolidate Soviet dominion over Eastern Europe and to perpetuate the frontiers established following World War II, thus forever dividing Germany and the two halves of Europe. This was confirmed in a statement issued from Moscow to the effect that "socialist states" would always remain in the socialist camp. This became known as the Brezhnev Doctrine. Many in the West thought Moscow's objectives also included undermining the cohesion of NATO and of the European Community. This view was only strengthened by Soviet General Secretary Brezhnev's revival in 1969 of an old Soviet proposal to convene an all-European security conference.

The Nixon administration began its term of office in January 1969. Nixon and his national security advisor, Henry Kissinger, adopted a policy toward the Soviet Union based on the principle that Moscow should be encouraged to believe that it had a vested interest in the status quo.[30] This was seen by the White House as the only realistic policy compatible with American interests, given the weakened international posture of the United States at that stage of the Vietnam War and the steady growth in Soviet military strength since Moscow's humiliation in the Cuban Missile Crisis in 1962. A European Security Conference that would do nothing more than legitimize the status quo in Europe was therefore compatible with a key premise of Nixon-Kissinger foreign policy, especially since the White House thought that West German chancellor Willy Brandt's Ostpolitik, aimed at normalizing relations with West Germany's eastern neighbors, seemed likely to permanently divide Germany anyway.[31]

West Germany's opening to the East (Ostpolitik) was the critical step in the process that led to the CSCE. Brandt saw his eastern treaties as transformational steps in Central and Eastern Europe, but he was counting on events in the long term to bear out his expectation. (Compare this with the Republic of Korea's "Sunshine Policy" or "engagement policy" vis-à-vis the DPRK during the presidency of Kim Dae Jung from 1998 to 2007.) In the short term, West Germany appeared to have given the Soviet Union and East Germany, in a bilateral framework, almost everything they could hope to get in the CSCE. But the new element in the CSCE, as opposed to Brandt's bilateral treaties with West Germany's neighbors, would be its multilateral character, giving it the quality of a surrogate peace treaty ending World War II. Importantly for engagement proponents, Ostpolitik lifted restraints from the other European countries in their own dealings in the East. This included, of course, taking a fresh look at the old Soviet idea of a European Security Conference.

The problem, as seen in Washington, was how to limit damage to American interests if a European Security Conference were ever held. There were two proposed solutions to this problem. One, favored in the White House, was to ensure that all serious security issues—those that might affect the US troop presence in Europe—were detached from the European Security Conference and that the conference itself become a nonevent. Separate negotiations on troop reductions would be set up to control the pace and timing of any eventual US troop withdrawals from Europe. The White House approach was not greatly at variance with Moscow's thinking about the conference. In the course of its drive for an All-European Conference in the months after the Czechoslovak invasion, Moscow made it clear that a few simple declarations would suffice for its purposes. The Warsaw Pact foreign ministers meeting in Prague on October 30–31, 1969, identified just two agenda items: nonuse of force and economic, technical, and scientific cooperation.

An All-European Conference[32] would accomplish some specific Soviet objectives as the State Department saw them at the time: recognition of the German Democratic Republic, acceptance of the status quo in Eastern Europe, and papering over the invasion of Czechoslovakia.[33]

And so, a second solution to the problem of limiting damage—favored by the State Department—was to counter Soviet demands for ratification of the territorial and political gains Moscow had made in Central and Eastern Europe in the aftermath of World War II with Western demands that would tend to neutralize the effects Moscow hoped would flow from a European Security Conference. At first, the Western idea of counterdemands focused only on negating the Brezhnev Doctrine of the limited sovereignty of "socialist states" that Moscow had invoked to justify the Warsaw Pact's invasion of Czechoslovakia in 1968. As 1969 wore on, the idea of another counterdemand began to take hold in several allied capitals. This idea was captured in the phrase "freer movement of people, ideas, and information" or simply "freer movement."

Moscow soon became aware from press reports and probably other sources that the North Atlantic Council was reviewing an extensive list of issues for negotiation with the East. The consistent Soviet stance was that the work program for the All-European Conference should be kept simple. Furthermore, while some East Europeans talked about a series of conferences, the typical Soviet view was that one conference would suffice.

Secretary of State William P. Rogers at this time thought that the best way to handle the Soviet proposal was to invent counterproposals.[34] Accordingly, the State Department authorized the US mission to the North Atlantic Council in Brussels to introduce a declaration on European security into the preparations for the December ministerial meeting. This was done on November 25, 1969, and resulted in the issuance of a "Declaration of the North Atlantic Council" on December 5, 1969. Paragraph 11 of the Declaration states:

> Allied governments consider that not only economic and technical but also cultural exchanges between interested countries can bring mutual benefit and understanding. In these fields more could be achieved by freer movement of people, ideas, and information between the countries of East and West.[35]

This provided the authorization for the US mission to NATO and the State Department from then on to push for a strong "freer movement" plank in allied positions in the CSCE. The declaration also acknowledged the possibility of eventually holding a general conference. Agreed-upon NATO criteria for judging the acceptability of a conference also were established:

- Progress on fundamental problems of European security in other forums;
- Participation of North American members of the alliance;
- Careful advance preparation and prospects of concrete results; and
- Assurance that a conference would not serve to ratify the division of Europe but instead would represent an effort to tackle the problems that separated the nations.

These criteria obviously were not in tune with White House thinking but they guided Department of State officials during the next three years of preparation for the CSCE.

National Security Advisor Henry Kissinger issued National Security Study Memorandum 138 on October 2, 1971. It asked for an interagency discussion of differing concepts of a Conference on European Security. The short deadline—November 1, 1971—did not allow much time for an in-depth study, and the report essentially endorsed State's position. In particular, the State Department's Bureau of European Affairs sought to emphasize the potential importance of a Conference on European Security in achieving long-term US objectives by including the following statement:[36]

To the extent the influence of the Western community can be extended east-
ward, common Western purposes are served. . . . Within the longer perspective of an emerging trans-Atlantic order, involving not only Western but
Eastern Europe, CES [Conference on European Security] assumes heightened potential relevance.

In negotiations with the Soviet leadership culminating in September
1972, the Americans agreed with the Soviets on the idea of parallel talks
on a European Security Conference and on troop reductions in Europe,
and specific dates were established for the beginning of the two negotiations.

NATO had conducted detailed consultations in Brussels regarding proposals for the CSCE since April 1969. At the conclusion of those efforts
following three years of discussions, the State Department was able to
report, with evident satisfaction, that:

> The US has taken the lead, during NATO consultations on CSCE issues, to
> develop the freer movement topic as a major Allied proposal. In the West
> the general belief is that European security will be enhanced by the gradual
> bridging of the divisions of Europe. Moreover, the West cannot accept the
> "legitimacy" of the political status quo in Eastern Europe. The freer move-
> ment proposal thus reasserts the Western interest in constructive, peaceful
> and liberalizing change, in contradistinction to Soviet emphasis on legitimiz-
> ing the status quo at the level of state-to-state relations.[37]

But when the multilateral preparatory talks on the CSCE began in Helsinki on November 22, 1972, the high-profile American posture on freer
movement abruptly switched to a behind-the-scenes role. From the beginning of the talks in Helsinki, it was clear that Soviet representatives
believed that the projected formal beginning of the CSCE in June 1973
was a done deal, not to be affected by questions of substance. They sought
and expected to receive American cooperation in making that happen.
John Maresca commented on this in his classic book on the CSCE, *To Helsinki*:

> While there was a vivid desire in the delegation and at the working level of
> the State Department to support the Western side, the officials concerned
> were afraid that if they attempted to put instructions in writing, Kissinger
> would not agree to a strong US position.[38]

The final agreement to include the human rights topic in the agenda of
the CSCE therefore depended on firm European leadership and a Western
consensus on what should be achieved in the CSCE. Both factors were
present; the former because the European nations wanted a success in

their newly created political consultations within the European Community framework, the latter because of three years of intense NATO consultations led by the United States. The European Community had essentially adopted the key elements of the program developed with NATO consultations.

On June 8, 1973, the participants in the Helsinki talks gave their collective agreement to the "Final Recommendations of the Helsinki Consultations." The next phase took place in Geneva. Even then, the outcome was not foreordained. The Nixon-Kissinger White House still did not share the views that American diplomats had been advocating since 1970 about the importance of human rights in the CSCE. In fact, Henry Kissinger made this painfully clear to the NATO allies in a meeting with Permanent Representatives to the North Atlantic Council at the Western White House in San Clemente, California, on June 30, 1973, shortly before the Geneva phase of the talks was to begin. As reported by European participants, he said, "Our only goal is now to prevent it from becoming a cosmic event which could be regarded by the public as a spectacular result." And later he added, "I do not believe the Soviet Union is going to be eased out of Eastern Europe by some sort of declaration. The sooner the conference is over the better."

A long and difficult negotiation resulted in the signing of the Helsinki Final Act on August 1, 1975.[39] For the United States, the Final Act was signed by Gerald Ford, who had become president upon Richard Nixon's resignation in August 1974. By the spring of 1975 it had become clear that the position initially advocated by the State Department had won the day, thanks in large part to the determination of West European negotiators, quietly backed by the Americans. But, ironically, Henry Kissinger, who became secretary of state in August 1973, finally was cast in the role of securing the human rights provisions in the Final Act. John Maresca tells the story in his book *To Helsinki*:

> Although Kissinger evidently found human rights issues largely irrelevant to superpower politics, it was he who, in Vienna in the spring of 1975, took up the remaining unresolved issues in Basket III (the human dimension) with Gromyko, thus impressing the Soviets with the need to make sufficient concessions in this area to make it possible for Western governments to accept a summit-level conclusion. This was one of the most important turning points in the Conference.[40]

The lessons for contemporary policy debate of this European experience are profound. At the heart of the Helsinki Final Act was the idea that Europe and North America are not merely thirty-five states with their sovereign rights but also millions of people with their own rights, needs, and aspirations. The promise of the Helsinki process was a community free of unnatural barriers and rich in diversity, a "Europe whole and free" as President George H. W. Bush later put it. Breaking down walls was a prelude to affirming and promoting common values—freedom of thought, conscience, and religion and the right to self-determination free from outside interference. That was long before social media introduced popular, not just state-sponsored options, into the global conversation.

A key element of the Final Act was that it required follow-up meetings, both to review implementation of its provisions and to expand the scope of cooperation. The first follow-up meeting, held in Belgrade, established the principle that the Helsinki Final Act was not a finished product but rather the beginning of a process. Subsequent review meetings firmly established the principle of accountability, and numerous meetings of experts widened the possibilities for cooperative relations envisaged in the accords of 1975. The bipolar order that had been imprinted on a divided Europe during the Cold War crumbled with the Berlin Wall in November 1989 and ended with the unification of Germany a year later. Twenty years after the signing of the Helsinki Final Act, the long-serving Soviet ambassador to the United States, Anatoly Dobrynin, wrote in his memoir *In Confidence*:

> Its ultimate reality was that it played a significant role in bringing about the long and difficult process of liberalization inside the Soviet Union and the nations of Eastern Europe. This in the end caused the fundamental changes in all these countries that helped end the Cold War.[41]

The European experience shows that adversaries can reach security agreements even when they do not share common values or common assumptions about the effect of the agreement they are negotiating. Engagement across ideological or other boundaries is essential. This implies a willingness to coexist and a readiness to treat adversaries as valid partners. So far, these conditions are lacking in the Middle East and Northeast Asia. In South Asia, the lingering suspicions after three wars make a wary coexistence a normal situation and one that is still not stable.

CAN OPENINGS TO PEACE BE ACHIEVED WITH SMALL STEPS?

Human rights progress was not the only achievement of the Final Act. A beginning also was made in making military cooperation a normal practice among adversaries. A category of cooperative security actions known as Confidence and Security Building Measures (CSBMs) was devised and systematically expanded in scope in the Helsinki Process. The Final Act contained some modest agreements for advance notification of military exercises, and in 1986 these were substantially expanded in the Stockholm Conference, a follow-up to the Helsinki Final Act, and in subsequent Review Conferences. These confidence-building measures dealt with conventional forces, not nuclear weapons, and did not change the military equations among the nations, although they helped avoid a war that no one wanted. Their main merit was that they gradually reinforced the idea that cooperation with adversaries was a legitimate and normal activity. They also gave smaller nations a larger voice in security measures than had been the case in earlier times, and they encouraged the habit of cooperation. An effort to negotiate confidence-building measures in other regions of the world would help to reinforce a habit of cooperation and to build momentum toward more transformative agreements.

In the Middle East, confidence-building measures of the type pioneered in Europe would be a major achievement if the parties could bring themselves to go this far. Conceivably, some transparency measures could be negotiated or some kind of security assurances could be devised in which outside powers might play a part. The transparency measures used in the Sinai when Israel withdrew from that area could be applied more broadly. These relied on sensors and overflights by US aircraft to warn against any developing signs of surprise attack.

In South Asia, Pakistan and India have negotiated confidence-building measures of various types aimed at avoiding miscalculations, some of them focused on nuclear sites. There is scope for much more in this area, with respect to both conventional and nuclear arms. For example, if India were willing to enter into a multilateral agreement on a nuclear test moratorium, like the statement of the five permanent members (China, France, Russia, the United Kingdom and Northern Ireland, and the United States) of the UN Security Council (UNSC) on September 15, 2016, Pakistan might follow.[42] Pakistan has already offered to join India in a bilateral test moratorium.[43] The same might be true for a declaration that production of fissile materials would not be used for weapons purposes. The permanent members of the UNSC essentially follow this policy norm as matters of national policies, and India and Pakistan might be willing to adopt the same posture in a joint declaration with them.

In Northeast Asia, there is a long history of discussion and negotiations with North Korea in various formats, and the issues are fairly well defined. Confidence-building measures have been proposed and were embedded in the 1992 Basic Agreement cited above.

It is quite possible that in Northeast Asia, the Middle East, or South Asia, progress in confidence-building measures in the military field could be made. This could encourage progress in the political and economic fields. The formula that could be adopted in each of these areas would be to propose a set of basic military confidence-building measures (CBMs) that would complement efforts to find nonmilitary areas for cooperation. In the Middle East and South Asia, cooperation in dealing with water shortages, for example, would be an important way of changing relationships. In Northeast Asia, economic and energy cooperation may be especially useful in supporting and sustaining progress in limiting North Korea's nuclear and missile programs.

ARE THERE GLOBAL AND REGIONAL SYNERGIES THAT CAN BE EXPLOITED?

Global agreements creating the conditions for a world without nuclear weapons will be difficult to accomplish while key regions of the world are beset by internal conflicts. Defusing those regional confrontations and taking steps toward cooperation, however modest, could contribute to progress worldwide towards a reduction in this nuclear threat.

The Euro-Atlantic Area. If regional nuclear wars became less likely, the entire world would step back from the brink. This is the contribution that the European Union has been making since its foundation nearly seventy years ago. Fragmentation of the European Union and a return to nationalism would remove one powerful disincentive to war in a key region of the world, and that has global implications. The long peace that has prevailed in Western Europe since World War II will probably not come to an end because of the current turbulence, but that assessment can no longer be taken as a given following conflict in Ukraine, Brexit, and the rise of populist parties across Europe. Europe appears to be moving from a condition of solid stability to a condition of metastability.

The Middle East, South Asia, and Northeast Asia. Regional negotiations in these areas could be enormously important in preventing nuclear war, but at the moment, that format has not shown much promise. So the synergies might work the other way in this case; global integration and global efforts to create the conditions for a world without nuclear weapons might compensate for the inability to reach regional settlements in these conflict-prone areas of the world because global agreements could encourage a resolution of differences in some regions.

For example, negotiations leading to limits on strategic nuclear forces have been almost exclusively the business of the United States and the Soviet Union/Russia. But when the paradigm of strategic nuclear negotiations dominated by the two biggest nuclear powers gives way to a multilateral format, as it must eventually, the potential for more direct involvement by regional groupings in this issue will rapidly come to the fore. There is a possibility, therefore, that successful negotiations on reducing the nuclear threat might encourage greater willingness to negotiate meaningfully at the regional level.

Vigorous, high-level negotiations on nuclear weapons among several of the most important states in the world could provide incentives for states in Europe, the Middle East, South Asia, and Northeast Asia to organize themselves in a way that will foster dialogue and ultimately, perhaps, genuine cooperation. The basic problem is the lack of trust among the nations in the conflict regions, which makes every issue a zero-sum game and makes external support suspect. Possibly a start can be made in building trust by agreeing on actions that would help citizens in adversarial states and that would be provided by a broad coalition of nations. There are shared problems in most regions—water shortages in the Middle East and South Asia, where climate change is drying up the sources of water supplies and, in Northeast Asia, energy and economic cooperation—which could only be definitively addressed through negotiations among adversaries but which could be set on the road to a solution by a global coalition.

A JOINT ENTERPRISE

If successes were achieved at the global level, could a joint enterprise that included regional and global powers have more promise? I think the answer is yes. Consider the following hypothetical scenarios involving South Asia:

1. On the bilateral level in South Asia, a variety of confidence-building measures between India and Pakistan are imaginable, focusing on developing the habit of cooperation and transparency. South Asia is a prime example of the need to change economic and political relations in parallel with engaging in security cooperation. South Asia is also badly in need of building momentum toward nuclear

restraint. The momentum is in the other direction now. The advantage of addressing such regional issues within the framework of a global institution might come into play in South Asia. India sees itself as in the same league as China, not Pakistan, and being an equal player in a joint enterprise with permanent members of the UN Security Council, thus minimizing the appearance of discrimination between India and the permanent UNSC members, should facilitate an India-Pakistan negotiation.

2. Pakistan has been blocking discussions of a cutoff of production of fissile material for use in nuclear bombs and warheads in the major existing disarmament forum, the Geneva-based Conference on Disarmament. But if invited to participate with other states possessing nuclear weapons in a new forum that convened periodically at the summit level, then Pakistan's response might be different. It would be harder to say no in a summit-level setting where other states, perhaps including India, were willing to commit to creating the conditions for a world without nuclear weapons.

3. If the leaders of several nations from around the world were to unite in establishing a joint enterprise aimed at creating the conditions for a world without nuclear weapons, they might agree on a work program that would take them toward that goal. That program might include an agenda item concerning limits on further production of nuclear weapons and reductions, or a freeze on deployed nuclear warheads.

Scenarios like these can be envisaged for other areas of the world. The bottom line is that policy makers should be looking for such synergies.

North Korea claims the status of a nuclear-weapon state, although other nations refuse to accept that status as a legal matter. Currently, it is refusing to recommit to a nuclear-weapon-free Korean Peninsula, a commitment Pyongyang was willing to make in the eras of Kim Il Sung and Kim Jong Il. Would Kim Jong Un, the grandson and son of those two leaders, be willing to commit to a nuclear-weapon-free Korean Peninsula in the context of a joint enterprise that included Japan, South Korea, Russia, China, and the United States? One cannot safely predict what Kim Jong Un's answer would be, but this option would be more likely to elicit a favorable reply than where things were left when the Six-Party Talks broke down.

In the Middle East, as part of a new forum that would include all of the permanent members of the UN Security Council plus Iran, Saudi Arabia, Egypt, Turkey, and Israel, agreements currently beyond reach might become possible. They include a set of confidence-building measures; a cutoff of production of fissile material for use in bombs and warheads;

and a ratified Comprehensive Nuclear Test Ban Treaty (CTBT). Experience suggests that incremental steps are more likely to build momentum toward eventual elimination of nuclear weapons than a commitment to do so instantly.

SUMMING UP

Despite political differences, under circumstances where all parties want, or are at least willing, to think about a change of some kind in the status quo, it is possible to reach cooperative security agreements that peacefully transform a region. Three essential factors need to exist and should be the basis for order-building diplomacy:

- A willingness to engage adversaries in gambling that security improvements are possible;
- An agenda that is broad enough to encompass the specific concerns of all major parties to a negotiation; and
- A commitment to include the welfare of people, not just states, in the agenda.

Are these factors present in South Asia, Northeast Asia, and the Middle East? Not yet, and they may never be, but the three "simple" factors cited above were the basis for success in transforming Europe and might also provide a compass for global and regional diplomacy elsewhere.

Second, the experience of regional disputes in South Asia, the Middle East, and Northeast Asia show that nuclear weapons do not create a stable environment but instead create tensions and stimulate rivalries that stand in the way of political settlements. Removing nuclear weapons from the equation cannot be accomplished as an isolated event because the nuclear rivalries have become embedded within the matrix of the dispute. A comprehensive approach is the only way to proceed.

Third, regional organizations and institutions are almost certainly necessary to sustain peace settlements, but a global framework is necessary to start the process and create the synergies necessary to build the momentum for regional cooperative security.

NOTES

1. For an analysis of this issue, see George P. Shultz and James E. Goodby, eds., *The War That Must Never Be Fought* (Stanford, CA: Hoover Institution Press, 2015), especially part I.

2. "Joint Declaration of South and North Korea on the Denuclearization of the Korean Peninsula," signed January 20, 1992, http://www.nti.org/; "Agreement on Reconciliation, Nonaggression and Exchanges And Cooperation Between the South and the North," entered into force February 19, 1992, http://nautilus.org/
.

3. The best account of this period is by three participants, Joel Wit, Daniel Poneman, and Robert Gallucci, *Going Critical* (Washington, DC: Brookings Institution Press, 2005).

4. "US-DPRK Agreed Framework," signed October 21, 1994, http://www.nti.org/.

5. William Perry, "The North Korean Policy Review: Triumph and Tragedy," in *My Journey at the Nuclear Brink* (Stanford, CA: Stanford University Press, 2015), 160–71.

6. "The Six-Party Talks at a Glance," *Arms Control Association*, https://www.armscontrol.org/factsheets/6partytalks.

7. "Text: Obama's Speech in Cairo," *New York Times* (June 4, 2009), http://www.nytimes.com/2009/06/04/us/politics/04obama.text.html.

8. Ankit Panda, "A Great Leap to Nowhere: Remembering the US-North Korea 'Leap Day' Deal," *The Diplomat* (February 29, 2016), http://thediplomat.com/2016/02/a-great-leap-to-nowhere-remembering-the-us-north-korea-leap-day-deal/. No text of an agreement was ever released.

9. "North Korea's 'Biggest' Nuclear Test Sparks Sanctions Push," *BBC* (September 10, 2016), http://www.bbc.co.uk/news/world-asia-37317782.

10. For Kim Jong Un's 2017 New Year's address, see Choe Sang-Hun, "Kim Jong-un Says North Korea Is Preparing to Test Long-Range Missile," *New York Times* (January 1, 2017), https://www.nytimes.com/2017/01/01/world/asia/north-korea-intercontinental-ballistic-missile-test-kim-jong-un.html?_r=0.

11. Terry Atlas, "Dealing with Russia and North Korea: An Interview with Siegfried Hecker," *Arms Control Association* (November 2016), https://www.armscontrol.org/ACT/2016_11/Features/Dealing-With-Russia-and-North-Korea-An-Interview-With-Siegfried-Hecker.

12. UN Resolution L.41, http://reachingcriticalwill.org/images/documents/Disarmament-fora/1com/1com16/resolutions/L41.pdf.

13. "First Nuclear Test at Pokhran in 1974," *Federation of American Scientists*, https://fas.org/nuke/guide/india/nuke/first-pix.htm.

14. Michael Laufer, "A. Q. Khan Nuclear Chronology," *Carnegie Endowment for International Peace* (September 7, 2005), http://carnegieendowment.org/2005/09/07/a.-q.-khan-nuclear-chronology.

15. Tim Weiner, "US and China Helped Pakistan Build Its Bomb," *International New York Times* (June 1, 1998), http://partners.nytimes.com/library/world/asia/060198pakistan-nuke-history.html.

16. Usman Ansari, "Fourth Pakistani Reactor Meets Long-Term Goal," *DefenseNews*, (January 19, 2015), http://www.defensenews.com/story/defense/policy-budget/warfare/2015/01/19/pakistan-reactor-nuclear-plutonium-fourth-isis-deterrent/22006509/.

17. Toby Dalton and George Perkovich, "Is a Pakistan-India War Just One Terrorist Attack Away?" *Herald* (January 23, 2017), http://herald.dawn.com/news/1153648.

18. Randeep Ramesh, "India Hands Mumbai Terror Attack Evidence to Pakistan," *Guardian*, (January 5, 2009), https://www.theguardian.com/world/2009/jan/05/mumbai-terror-attacks-india-pakistan.

19. "Kashmir Attack: India 'Launches Strikes Against Militants,'" *BBC* (September 30, 2016).

20. Walter C. Ladwig III, "A Cold Start for Hot Wars? The Indian Army's New Limited War Doctrine," *International Security* 32, no. 3 (Winter 2007/2008).

21. Toby Dalton and George Perkovich, "India's Nuclear Options and Escalation Dominance," Carnegie Endowment for International Peace, May 19, 2016, http://carnegieendowment.org/2016/05/19/india-s-nuclear-options-and-escalation-dominance-pub-63609.

22. Paul Kerr, "Bush's Claims About Iraq's Nuclear Program," *Arms Control Today/Arms Control Association* (September 1, 2003), https://www.armscontrol.org/print/1361.

23. "CIA's Final Report: No WMD Found in Iraq," *NBC News*, April 25, 2005, http://www.nbcnews.com/id/7634313/ns/world_news-mideast_n_africa/t/cias-final-report-no-wmd-found-iraq/#.WK9ZRjvyuUk.

24. IAEA Board of Governors, "Implementation of the NPT Safeguards Agreement in the Islamic Republic of Iran," November 15, 2004, https://www.iaea.org/sites/default/files/gov2004-83.pdf.

25. Timeline of the Joint Comprehensive Plan of Action (JCPOA), http://jcpoatimeline.csis.org/.

26. Olli Heinonen and Simon Henderson, "Nuclear Kingdom: Saudi Arabia's Atomic Ambitions," *The Washington Institute for Near East Policy* (May 27, 2014), http://www.washingtoninstitute.org/policy-analysis/view/nuclear-kingdom-saudi-arabias-atomic-ambitions.

27. David Makovsky, "The Silent Strike: How Israel Bombed a Syrian Nuclear Installation and Kept It Secret," *The New Yorker* (September 17, 2012).

28. The United States signed a nuclear cooperation agreement with the United Arab Emirates on January 15, 2009, which is called the "gold standard" for nuclear safeguards.

29. This narrative is adapted from papers I have presented in several forums in slightly different versions. This text is drawn mainly from chapter 2 of James Goodby, *Europe Undivided: The New Logic of Peace in US-Russian Relations* (Washington, DC: US Institute of Peace, 1998).

30. Note, for example, Nixon's definition of "the first stage of detente: to involve Soviet interests in ways that would increase their stake in international stability and the status quo." From *RN: The Memoirs of Richard Nixon* (New York: Grosset & Dunlop, 1978), 618.

31. On the effect of Ostpolitik, Henry Kissinger wrote, "I thought Ostpolitik was more likely to lead to a permanent division of Germany than to healing its breach." From Henry Kissinger, *White House Years* (Boston: Little, Brown and Co., 1979), 411.

32. Talking paper left at the Department of State by Soviet Ambassador Anatoly Dobrynin on November 19, 1969.

33. Memorandum of conversation of November 28, 1969, between Assistant Secretary of State Martin Hillenbrand and Finnish Ambassador Olavi Munkki.

34. US Department of State memorandum of conversation of November 12, 1969, between Secretary Rogers and FRG Defense Minister Helmut Schmidt.

35. In speaking of "human rights" in the Helsinki Final Act of 1975, the freer movement provisions are the operational elements and the human rights principle in the declaration of principles is the statement of a general obligation. The specific obligations have figured prominently in all of the compliance reviews since the first review meeting in Belgrade.

36. The description of this report is from a text sent by the US Department of State (E. J. Streator) to various agencies for final clearance on October 30, 1971. This text already had been discussed and revised in the interagency process.

37. Memorandum from Bureau of European Affairs (EUR/RPM: Ralph J. McGuire) to CSCE Task Force Working Group on Freer Movement. Subject: Public Affairs Guidance for CSCE—Freer Movement of People, Ideas and information. November 19, 1972.

38. John J. Maresca, *To Helsinki: The Conference on Security and Cooperation in Europe 1973–1975* (Durham, NC: Duke University Press, 1985), 44.

39. The Helsinki Final Act and other documents recording agreements on the Helsinki Process are available on the website of the Organization for Security and Cooperation in Europe, http://www.osce.org/helsinki-final-act.

40. Maresca, *To Helsinki: The Conference on Security and Cooperation.*

41. Anatoly Dobrynin, *In Confidence: Moscow's Ambassador to America's Six Cold War Presidents (1962–1986)* (New York: Crown, 1995), 347.

42. Joint Statement from the Nuclear-Weapons States at the 2016 Washington, DC P5 Conference, Nuclear Security Working Group, September 16, 2016, http://nuclearsecurityworkinggroup.org/joint-statement-from-the-nuclear-weapons-states-at-the-2016-washington-dc-p5-conference/. The P5 reaffirmed their own moratorium on nuclear explosions.

43. "Pakistan Reiterates Offer for Bilateral Non-testing of Nuclear Weapons with India," *Times of Islamabad* (September 10, 2016), https://timesofislamabad.com/pakistan-reiterates-offer-bilateral-non-testing-nuclear-weapons-india/2016/09/01/.

FIVE

Global Security Cooperation

An Agenda for Early Action

We shall see how absolute is the need of a broad path of international
action pursued by many states in common across the years, irrespec-
tive of the ebb and flow of national politics.

—Winston Churchill

Nuclear confrontations in regions where disputes have simmered for
years are apt to persist in the absence of some external input. Accordingly, in the previous chapter, the analysis of synergies that would promote progress in cooperative security, both globally and regionally,
concluded that although synergies can work in both directions, global
agreements are more likely to stimulate movements toward settlements
at the regional level than are regional settlements likely to promote global
agreements.

The analysis also suggested that small steps toward security cooperation in regions like Northeast Asia, the Middle East, and South Asia could
promote progress that would make political settlements more likely. For
that reason, every effort should be made to look for openings to even
minor cooperative security agreements rather than give up on resolving
regional disputes.

In this chapter, we will turn to global security cooperation, meaning
bilateral agreements between major powers like the United States, China,
and Russia, each a permanent member of the UN Security Council, and
India and Japan, as well. We will also address multilateral agreements of
a geographic scope that justify the adjective "global," such as UN-
sponsored negotiating forums or former President Obama's Nuclear
Security Summits.

Geopolitical rivalries stand in the way of cooperative security at the
global level as do geography, history, and differing perceptions of basic

national interests. The ongoing transition in the international system adds other complications. The governments of the world's major nations will, if they are wise and agile enough, do their best to shape that transition. Whether they can find enough common ground to work together in shaping a transition to a twenty-first-century global security commons is an open question.

A global commons cannot be built on trade alone. It will have to include such joint activities as those addressing climate change and nuclear threats. An expression of a global security commons and of a mechanism for managing it could be a coalition of nations willing to work together in a sustained fashion to create the conditions for a world free of nuclear weapons. Working together to build a new global architecture for jointly managing the global nuclear threat requires not only negotiating reductions in numbers of weapons but also creating systems for managing and sustaining a world without nuclear weapons. Included in this task are: building and maintaining a fissile materials security system; a fuel cycle management system; a verification system; and an enforcement system.

Thinking afresh about defining a global commons relevant to twenty-first-century needs has been delayed for too long. A commons is no longer just a common area where a village's sheep graze; nor is it, as traditionally defined, just those areas which are not under the sovereign control of any one nation, such as space and the high seas. People living in the age of globalism, united or divided by the Internet and social media, have a set of interests, some of which, like self-preservation, are long-standing and common to all humanity. They aspire to create a better and safer world for their descendants. The global security commons now includes an array of ecological developments that present threats to humanity's survival and to the survival of nations. Pandemics are another existential threat.

The effects of the use of nuclear weapons clearly could portend the end of the human race if used on the scale contemplated during the Cold War. Today, large populations live as potential targets of unstable or antagonistic nations already possessing nuclear weapons or moving to develop this capability. Current policies nearly everywhere in the world only delay the use of nuclear weapons, thus endangering future generations. Shared basic interests in meeting such challenges can be thought of as the elements for the commons of all nations. So the global security commons must be managed and sustained across generations in the interests of all nations and the whole of humanity. The key to building momentum in that direction is leadership, and that is lacking.

UNITED STATES AND RUSSIA

As this book is being written, it is not yet clear whether the Trump administration intends to pursue cooperative security agreements that focus on nuclear weapons. The president's attitude toward Russia has been quite positive, but negotiations between the two countries on nuclear issues effectively broke down after 2010 and it is uncertain whether they can be revived. Very little can be accomplished in building a global security commons unless the current tensions in US-Russian relations are eased in some way.[1]

The first step in devising guidelines for a future US strategy is to frame the issues correctly. For example, it would be wrong to think that Russia is the origin of all the problems in the enormously complex mix of ethnic groups that inhabit the regions around its borders and also within that sprawling country. True, Moscow is an enabler of separatist movements in eastern Ukraine, Georgia, Moldova, and elsewhere, and it seems to find that divide-and-conquer policies suit its security needs. But it would be simplistic to think that if Moscow suddenly became cooperative, all would be well. Because of the emotions and the long histories involved in all the disputes in what President Putin calls "former Soviet space," it will take time before trust takes root between central governments and those ethnic groups inclined either toward independence or toward a closer relationship with Russia. The diplomacy of "gardening"—patient and prolonged engagement—is required in such cases.[2]

Framing the issues correctly also means an accurate assessment of where Putin may be heading and where Russia might be able and willing to follow him. Putin's actions in Ukraine and his domestic crackdown on dissent are certainly reminiscent of the Cold War, or worse. Some have compared this period to the years leading up to World War II. But Putin's Russia is not Stalin's Russia, and the world of 2017 is notable for the many ways in which nations and the international system itself are changing under the impact of globalization, technology, and the rise of social media.

Seen in the light of megatrends dominating the global landscape today, Putin's efforts to turn back the clock are unlikely to succeed, no matter how fervently he evokes nostalgia for Russia's historical borders. The people-to-people links between Russia and the West and an unparalleled access to information in all nations will not easily be severed, despite fake news, hacking, and trolls.

One interpretation of events is that Russia is undergoing the trauma of a lost empire. Like other postimperial powers, Moscow is having trouble adjusting to its changed status. It naturally believes that it should have a privileged position in the nations that once were part of the czarist, and then Soviet, empires, but President Putin also thinks that he should be entitled to exclude political or other changes in neighboring countries of which he disapproves. But no more than other European nations could reestablish their "blue-water" empires will Moscow be able to recreate the Soviet Union or the Russian empire on the land mass of Eurasia.

Not all of what we are seeing is traceable to the long recessional march from empire, as shaped by Russia's particular experiences. Putin also is responding to a general resentment among Russians that despite their contributions to European civilization, despite all the sacrifices Russians made in World War II, and despite their having overthrown communism and embraced democracy, the West has never treated them with the respect and friendship they have earned and deserved. Their interests are ignored, their sensitivities scorned.

Notwithstanding this situation, and even because of it, American policy makers need to balance the twin American imperatives of good working relations with Russia and the long-term interest in encouraging democracy and freedom throughout the Euro-Atlantic community. In principle, the two imperatives should be compatible, especially within a policy framework designed to promote a Euro-Atlantic security community, including Russia, based on common values and a broad sense of a common identity. This should be a North Star for US policy, a multigenerational strategy, as containment was during the Cold War; and it is a positive, inclusionary vision, worthy of the West. A step on the way to that would be to include Russia, when it is ready, in a closer consultative arrangement than now exists, a concert-like approach.

If this strategy is pursued, the political changes that already have appeared in "post-Soviet space" and those yet to come in Russia will eventually succeed in transforming the frozen political landscape with its heated emotions lying not far beneath the surface. The interrupted march toward a Europe that is peaceful, undivided, and democratic will be resumed, and Russia ultimately will join it. But this is not Putin's vision of the future. He has left no doubt about this by embracing and, to some extent, creating an ideology based on right-wing principles that align him with Central Asia and with right-wing populist parties in Europe.

Realism requires an understanding that this situation, plus internal conditions in Russia and Moscow's policies toward its former dominions, is likely to stand in the way of its full inclusion in a Euro-Atlantic community for a long time to come. Events in Ukraine and Putin's crackdown on Russian dissent have underlined this.

Still, at a time when the direction of US policy is uncertain, a magnetic north for a policy compass that easily could become confused and directionless in the face of conflicting interests is a requirement for a successful long-term strategy. Bringing a stable peace to the Euro-Atlantic community is a worthy goal, and failure to seek Russia's ultimate inclusion in it, even as a distant prospect, would slow down political change across the region and erect new walls, thereby weakening the united international response to near-term challenges to humanity that is so badly needed.

Preventive diplomacy, crisis management, and order-building diplomacy all need to be deployed to meet the current problems created by Putin's actions in Europe. Resorting to the mechanisms established to support the undertakings of the Helsinki Final Act will help. Reasserting the validity of the vision of Euro-Atlantic relations held forth by the Final Act should be an absolutely bedrock policy for the United States, no matter what broader alternative strategy Washington chooses to pursue. The use of new communications methods now available through social media should be a part of the effort. It is in tune with the emphasis on people, not just states, in the Final Act itself.

There is no question that the North Atlantic Alliance, backed by American conventional and nuclear forces and supported by the modus vivendi that existed during the Cold War between the West and the Soviet Union, was a force for stability and peace. Deterrence worked then because both sides were willing to let it work, but times have changed.

Today's circumstances are very different and very dangerous because there is no clear modus vivendi that governs relations between the West and Russia in Europe or anywhere else. Russia appears to have adopted and pursued an aggressive strategy based on principles of "hybrid warfare" in which military force is blended with political and economic intimidation, and with disinformation, in order to achieve results. Russian spokesmen have made it clear that nuclear weapons are a part of this strategy. When combined with other tools of hybrid warfare, like cyberwar methods, this strategy presents a grave risk to global peace and stability.

If some new version of the Cold War modus vivendi between the West and Moscow could be put in place, it almost certainly would be accomplished in the same way as the Cold War understandings were reached: through tacit agreements rather than treaties. The Cold War modus vivendi was based on a division of Europe into what amounted to spheres of influence. Moscow's spokesmen, and President Vladimir Putin in particular, have made it clear for many years now that Russia sees "former Soviet space" as its sphere of interest.

In the past, other imperial powers also had a special interest in their former imperial territories in Asia, Africa, and the Middle East, but these "possessions" challenged that arrangement, just as Ukraine, Georgia, and other former Soviet Republics do today. In any case, spheres of influence are not consistent with an open framework for international cooperation, so the potential for conflict will exist until either (1) Russia and the West integrate in some form; or (2) the West and Moscow reach an understanding on a mutual accommodation of interests in Russia's neighborhood; or (3) a global cooperative security regime is established. In the many years it will likely take for an incremental process to produce one outcome or another, thus creating a new modus vivendi, the existential threat of nuclear war will continue to exist, including in Europe, which just after the end of the Cold War was the world's most promising area for regional cooperation between Russia and the West.

A GLOBAL CONCERT OF NATIONS?

Avoiding competition and enhancing cooperation was the idea behind the "Concert of Europe" in the nineteenth century. The experience has relevance today. Russia and the United States may never be as close as the United States and its fellow liberal democracies can be because their values may diverge. Nevertheless, a "concert" system that includes both Russia and the United States should be a realistic goal whenever current issues over the political order in Europe are resolved, and perhaps as a part of that settlement.

In 1991, writing in *The Washington Quarterly*, I said that "there is and will be a common set of rules by which the Soviet Union, North America, and the European states pursue their international goals."

I had in mind the Helsinki Final Act when I mentioned a "common set of rules" and I saw the signatory states "as comprising a single society of states within which to work for ways of reinforcing order."

I saw this society of states through the lens of concert diplomacy, as in the Concert of Europe after the Napoleonic wars. The essence of the idea was that great powers should forswear unilateral action and work to achieve common policies much as the UN Security Council was supposed to work.[3]

In 1999, I wrote in an article in *Brookings Review*[4] that

> After centuries of war in Europe, historical experience does not encourage hopes for a stable peace but . . . a strategy aimed at making a stable peace in Europe must be aimed at creating something akin to a security community, that is, a single security space throughout Europe, including Russia.

With globalization then rapidly advancing, I also wrote that "an American equilibrium strategy must deal with both ends of Eurasia simultaneously. Disconnected policies for Europe and for Asia—

compartmentalization, in effect, is not compatible with globalization, which is here to stay, or with a coherent national strategy."

I also cited the European Union, Russia, China, and Japan as the big entities on which, together with the United States, a stable peace depended.

As events have moved on in recent years, a concert based on North America, the European Union, Russia, China, India, and Japan might work. This is similar to the UN Security Council plus Japan, India, and Germany, so enlarging the permanent membership of the Security Council would be an effective though very problematic way of institutionalizing a global concert. Such a grouping would be similar to the one that joined with Iran in negotiating the Iran nuclear deal, so the idea of a North American, Asian, and European Concert of Nations focused on international security cooperation has some precedents.

This is not exactly the same as a security community, which might be less structured and more focused in one geographic region. A security community continues to be an idea worth discussing in Euro-Atlantic relations. As recently as 2012, before the crisis over Ukraine erupted, European and American statesmen talked quite enthusiastically about this.[5]

THE ORDER-BUILDING IMPACT OF
NUCLEAR AGREEMENTS

Nuclear weapons present the most vivid example of how interstate relations are influenced by lethal weapons; experience in Russia-US relations suggests that a stable peace cannot be achieved between two nations while a nuclear competition exists between them. The peace will be conditional. In contrast, working at cooperation with the support of other concerned nations can alter perceptions on the wisdom of having nuclear weapons, as happened after 1986 in the US-Soviet/Russian case. Existential issues common to humanity can more readily be solved in a world where the nuclear status quo has been successfully challenged and a decisive turn in international relationships has been made. These issues will not be solved in an "all against all" Hobbesian world of perpetual conflict based on narrow self-interest.

An advantage of the nuclear project is that it also highlights a number of unresolved international problems, some of them regional, which would have to be addressed in creating the conditions for a world without nuclear weapons. It also facilitates a comprehensive approach that provides more confidence and assurances of stability at many levels, not just in nuclear relationships. This methodology would show that order-building diplomacy is key in successfully managing all the existential challenges that need to be addressed within a global security commons. And so cooperation would be shown to be superior to competition as a way of creating a global security commons.

The negotiations with Iran that led to an agreement to restrain Iran's nuclear programs are an example of this approach. In my view, the agreement, if it is to be ultimately successful, must lead to a changed, more cooperative security situation in the Middle East.[6] Otherwise, it will fail. There are other cases where this nuclear approach might work. One is the North Korean problem in Northeast Asia; the other is as a possible element of a regional settlement of the civil war in Syria.

GLOBAL-REGIONAL INTERACTION

In these days, big powers cannot dictate to the less powerful, even if spheres of interest policies were to be revived. The days of big powers deciding and small powers accepting are on their way out. But there can be, and should be, a place for powerful nations to act as role models and catalysts and facilitators. In the following pages, this kind of activity will be explored.

Northeast Asia

For the United States, the basic goal has been to persuade North Korea to proceed with the dismantlement of its nuclear-weapons program. This will require engagement with Pyongyang, but this has been missing for several years. Only through engagement can a "soft landing" from the present high level of tension be achieved. As North Korea's neighbor, China is focusing its attention on the disaster of a total breakdown of North Korean society and what that might mean for China, while Washington's principal focus is on the potential regional and global disaster of North Korea becoming a nuclear-weapon state with the same status as India and Pakistan.[7] Can these two views and sets of objectives be reconciled? Probably, but it will require the United States to engage in direct, high-level negotiations with North Korea as well as with China. Against this background, what should be the guiding principles of US policy?

First, and at a minimum, the United States should have the strategic objective of deterring and, if possible, reducing the military threat that North Korea poses to its neighbors and to the United States, not to mention the threats to world peace that North Korean nuclear and missile exports could generate. The United States also should have an interest in transformative diplomacy in the region.

It may sound fanciful even to speak of the possibilities for transformative diplomacy in the context of North Korea, but the tides of history are running against governments like those in Pyongyang. True, nationalism is on the march in many parts of the world, but the DPRK's system is not just nationalistic, it is totalitarian—in spades. Naturally enough, the regime in Pyongyang will resist reform, for their leaders fear loss of control. They also fear the loss of being a society distinct from that of the South, which justifies the perpetuation of their rule. They saw what happened to East Germany, which almost overnight was absorbed into West Germany once Communist rule in East Berlin ended. But this should not deter the United States and its allies from pursuing policies that will induce change.

Second, the United States, if it wishes to exert leadership in this area, needs to be more strategically active; it must end the policy of "strategic patience" it pursued during most of the Obama administration. The Trump administration has spoken of engagement with North Korea, but, as of this writing, has delegated that task to China.

Third, a concept of what a peace system for the Korean Peninsula would look like is a necessary component of an engagement policy. Even if the prospect of negotiating a modest first step with North Korea seems remote, the United States and its friends have to stand for something positive.

And fourth, a long-term vision for the Korean Peninsula and Northeast Asia is needed. Is it going to be a kind of updated hub-and-spoke system, in which a dominant power maximizes its influence through a web of bilateral connections, or should it be something more multilateral, and therefore more responsive to present realities?

The potential for transformative diplomacy in Northeast Asia is enormous, including new architecture for security and cooperation in Northeast Asia. A permanent multilateral mechanism in Northeast Asia, perhaps derived from the experience of the Six-Party Talks, would include Russia, China, Japan, and North and South Korea, as well as the United States. It could be a much-needed agent for change. A multilateral organization is not a panacea; many sensitive issues will continue to be handled through other channels. But the present pattern is clearly not sufficient to lead the nations of the region to a stable peace.

Replacing the 1953 Korean War Armistice Agreement with a US, ROK, China, DPRK interim agreement on regulating military deployments and activities in and around the Korean Peninsula could be an important step, especially in the context of a North Korean acceptance of the goal of a nuclear-weapon-free zone in Northeast Asia that would include Japan and South Korea, as well as North Korea. This interim agreement would not be a peace treaty. Relations are not yet mature enough for that. However, it could define borders and provide a four-party consultative mechanism between North and South Korea, China, and the United States—those nations most directly concerned with the Armistice Agreement.

The Middle East

Arms control obviously has been a daunting challenge even for governments that have attempted it in circumstances much more favorable than those currently prevailing in the Middle East. Once a settlement of the civil war in Syria has been reached, relatively small steps might be achievable. There would be an advantage for all parties concerned to try for a breakthrough in the area of transparency—that is, less secrecy about military activities.

Transparency measures in Europe have been expanded and strengthened over the years. Since 1986, they have included on-site inspection in Russia up to the Urals. Under the terms of the most recent agreements, data about changes in equipment holdings are exchanged, visits to corroborate these data are permitted, and defense budget information is exchanged. Military chiefs of staff have held fruitful discussions about military doctrine.

But not all lessons about transparency come from the European experience. Some highly sophisticated transparency measures operated in the Sinai Peninsula shortly after the end of the 1973 October War. Within weeks of the signing of the November 11, 1973, cease-fire agreement between Israel and Egypt, the United States had facilitated a series of transparency measures, including the creation of limited-force zones, inspections by UN forces, and air reconnaissance by US aircraft, even though both countries remained in a state of war.[8] In addition, after 1974, UN forces managed on-site challenge inspections of Israeli and Syrian forces in the Golan Heights, despite the fact that these two countries remained at war with one another.

GLOBALIZED NUCLEAR NEGOTIATIONS

In addition to global-regional interactions, the major nations could cooperate in building a security system that would have both a global and a regional impact. The infrastructure that is needed to build momentum for a serious push to establish a global cooperative security regime in the nuclear realm is currently missing. The following is a description of mechanisms that could help to create the essential infrastructure.

1. INITIATE A NUCLEAR SECURITY SUMMIT DEDICATED TO CREATING THE CONDITIONS FOR A WORLD WITHOUT NUCLEAR WEAPONS.

During President Obama's two terms in office, four summit meetings were held with the aim of improving the security of fissile material and nuclear-related technology globally.[9] Fifty or more heads of governments attended each summit meeting. Over the course of the four meetings, improvements in several areas were put into effect, some by multinational agreement, and many by national decisions. These summit meetings left the world a safer place but also left governments around the world recognizing that much more needs to be done. The meetings helped to create the conditions for a world without nuclear weapons by making proliferation of nuclear weapons less likely.

These Nuclear Security Summits could be a model for summits focused even more directly on creating the conditions for a world without nuclear weapons. Like the original Nuclear Security Summits, these meetings should include both states that are nuclear armed and those that are not. The first such meeting could issue a communiqué stating the determination of the leaders to work together to dismantle, step by step, the world's arsenals of nuclear weapons and laying down the conditions that would have to be met to achieve the ultimate goal.

Their communiqués would be accompanied by a work plan, which would commit the nations to a series of steps leading to a reduction in nuclear weapons by those who had them and the acceptance of safeguards by those nations that did not have nuclear weapons, similar to measures included in the Joint Comprehensive Plan of Action (JCPOA) with Iran.[10] In addition, a list of steps those participants in the proposed meetings were prepared to take immediately, as matters of national policy, would be included with the documentation.[11]

2. ESTABLISH A NEW ORGANIZATION FOR DISCUSSION OF NUCLEAR DISARMAMENT AND NONPROLIFERATION THAT RECOGNIZES THE COLLECTIVE RESPONSIBILITY OF ALL NATIONS FOR CREATING THE CONDITIONS FOR A WORLD WITHOUT NUCLEAR WEAPONS.

Whether or not a new version of the Nuclear Security Summits ever materializes, periodic summit meetings will be necessary to sustain top-level engagement, to make key decisions to iron out any difficulties that arise, and to chart a course for the future. And a permanent organization will be necessary to carry the work forward. No existing organization is capable of doing this. The UN's Committee on Disarmament has been moribund for years. The closest thing there is to such an organization is the Open-Ended Working Group recently set up in the UN framework to promote the work of the Non-Proliferation Treaty Review Meetings.[12]

On October 27, 2016, the First Committee of the UN General Assembly adopted a resolution (Resolution L.41) calling for negotiation of a treaty that would "prohibit nuclear weapons, leading towards their total elimination."[13] With the exception of North Korea, no state possessing nuclear weapons supported the resolution. An option that may have been opened up by this vote is that of convening a parallel meeting to discuss how total elimination would be achieved. Conceivably, such a group could mature into an authoritative organ for international decision making.

The simplest way to create a global cooperative security forum less focused on nuclear weapons might be to organize, on a global scale, a consultative mechanism similar to that of the Conference on Security and Co-operation in Europe (CSCE). Alternatively, regional organizations could be asked to send representatives to establish a global forum for cooperative security.

3. Practice cooperation.

Nuclear deterrence ultimately should go the way of the horse cavalry, but in the interim, greater clarity regarding national intentions could prevent misunderstandings and miscalculations. The permanent members of the UN Security Council have developed a program of consultations on nuclear matters in the past few years. Their report of September 15, 2016, showed that while relatively sensitive defense policies are now being discussed, the critical issue of nuclear-weapon-use doctrines does not attract the same degree of attention.[14] It would not be much of a stretch to get from where the P5 is now to the point where national nuclear-use policies could be the subject of consultations. This would include explanations of the conditions that might oblige national leadership to consider using nuclear weapons.

Within the successor organization to the CSCE—the Organization for Security and Co-operation in Europe (OSCE)—and also within the North Atlantic Treaty Organization (NATO), international consultations regarding defense policies have been conducted for many years. In the case of NATO, this has included intensive consultations about the purposes of nuclear weapons, concluding that these should be used only as a last resort.[15] Consultations within the OSCE have focused on conventional forces and broad defense policies.

There is ample precedence, in short, for consultations among nuclear-armed states for the purpose of avoiding the war that no one wants. In the context of a coalition of countries willing to work together for a world without nuclear weapons, similar consultations would be beneficial and should be initiated.

Each of the current nuclear-armed states faces unique domestic and international circumstances, so in the early phases of a transition to a nuclear-free world or region, caution about such consultations would be expected. A minimum, but important, achievement would be missile de-targeting, even recognizing its inherent unverifiability. In recent years, Russia and the United States have agreed on policies of de-targeting, meaning that during normal peacetime conditions, ballistic missile systems armed with nuclear weapons should be targeted on open ocean areas to prevent any possibility of an accidental firing of a missile aimed at the national territories of either Russia or the United States. A far more ambitious goal of restricting prompt launch capabilities in normal peacetime conditions should be on the agenda for early action.

4. Formalize policy statements of the Permanent Members of the Security Council (the P5).

The Non-Proliferation Treaty (NPT) Review Conferences prompted discussions concerning the P5 because the 2010 report of the Review Conference laid out an elaborate plan of action to which the P5 decided to respond in a coordinated fashion. Their report to the 2015 NPT Review Conference contained many useful ideas, including their joint statement regarding the continuance of each nation's unilateral moratorium on nuclear testing and their readiness to engage in negotiations on a fissile material cutoff treaty.

This document could readily be augmented by other P5 assurances, such as a coordinated statement regarding a joint moratorium on nuclear test explosions, on not producing fissile material for use in nuclear explosive devices, or on not producing fissile material at all. A statement like this could be subscribed to by other nations and become the core of a renewed commitment to nonproliferation, pending the negotiation of legally binding treaties. For example, a number of nuclear-armed states, not just the P5, might agree that the sole purpose of their nuclear arms is to deter the use of nuclear weapons by other nations. That agreement might be codified in a joint statement accepted by all of these nations.

What is the value of joint statements that do not require verification mechanisms? The idea is to encourage the habit of cooperation as a transitional arrangement en route to rigorously monitored and enforced agreements. Such measures would be designed to induce all nuclear-armed states to join in the first steps on the road to eliminating nuclear weapons and to make the world a safer place right away. But these measures can also be like canaries in a coal mine—alerting nations to any malevolent intentions of partners in this coalition of the willing. Lack of progress toward more verifiable measures of restraint would be a strategic warning. Success in such an effort, on the other hand, would lend momentum to the movement toward cooperative security.

OLD WINE IN NEW BOTTLES

The cooperative measures described in the following pages are examples of agreements that generally have been accepted by major nations but never implemented because of resistance at one level or another. They are cited as useful and practical steps that nations inclined to make a determined effort to create a safer nuclear regime should be able to take fairly quickly.

1. MISSILE DEFENSE

Some quite ambitious ideas that were advanced decades ago by the Reagan administration were never adopted. These include an imaginative plan conceived by Paul Nitze whereby defense against nuclear attacks would be built up as offensive forces were drawn down. President Reagan supported ballistic missile defenses as a safeguard against rogue states or cheating, arguing that this would be necessary even if the United States and the Soviet Union were able to eliminate all their nuclear-armed missiles.

At that time—the mid-1980s—the technology of ballistic missile defense was not so far advanced as to make Nitze's plan a feasible proposition. Even today, the enormous destructive power of a single nuclear warhead means that a missile defense would have to be almost foolproof to avert terrific damage to the nation under attack. That is not possible in an attack with large numbers of missiles equipped with multiple independently targetable reentry vehicles (MIRVs), decoys, or both. Even attacks by very few ballistic missiles with nuclear warheads, especially missiles that have sophisticated means for overcoming defenses, remain difficult to counter. Other possibilities such as stealth cruise missiles and boost-glide vehicles present almost insuperable problems for a defender. But a soundly based cooperative ballistic missile system between two or three countries could contribute to confidence building as nuclear forces are reduced.

2. EARLY WARNING

Less ambitious cooperative security measures also have been discussed and agreed upon in US-Russia negotiations, both at the official level and in Track II (informal) discussions. The potential for useful collaborations in early-warning information is evident since neither side benefits from a case of mistaken identification of an attack. Sharing information about attacks by third countries also could be useful in the US-Russia context in averting a catalytic war; that is, a US-Russia war triggered by an attack on one or the other by a third party, conceivably even a terrorist organization.

Despite these evident advantages, and despite a declaration by presidents Bush and Putin in 2002 that their nations would collaborate in early warning and ballistic missile defense, the level of confidence between the United States and Russia—even a quarter of a century after the collapse of the Soviet Union and the end of the Cold War—has never been high enough to follow through with a joint early-warning or defense system. When political conditions permit, this is one of the areas of cooperative security that the United States and Russia should revisit, perhaps with other nations, in a joint enterprise to create the conditions for a world without nuclear weapons.

3. Security Assurances

Assurances to nations that have accepted non-nuclear-weapon status under the terms of the Non-Proliferation Treaty (NPT) have been a part of that regime for many years. The basic assurance provides that a nuclear-weapon state will not use nuclear weapons against a state that has forsworn nuclear weapons. This is known as a negative assurance, whereas a positive assurance offers support (although ambiguous) to nations subjected to a nuclear attack or the threat of such an attack.

This is certainly an area that could be expanded in a protocol to the NPT or offered to adherents to a nuclear-weapon-free zone. Although welcomed by non-nuclear-weapon states, previous statements regarding assurances have been widely regarded as having little value in real-world situations.[16] They could, however, be the basis for serious negotiations on stronger assurances in regional peace settlements.

4. The Comprehensive Test Ban Treaty: An Iconic Agreement

Here is how a former Chairman of the US Joint Chiefs of Staff, General John Shalikashvili, US Army, assessed the importance of the comprehensive test ban treaty. Though written in 2001, his words are just as relevant today as they were then, perhaps even more so.

> The Test Ban Treaty is not an isolated measure operating in a vacuum. Rather, it is an integral and inseparable part of our national non-proliferation

strategy. An effective strategy must include the skillful use of a variety of political, diplomatic, economic , and military responses tailored for particular proliferation problems. This requires meticulous coordination among the relevant Executive Branch agencies, steady bipartisan support from Congress, and close cooperation with other countries. Only the United States has both a compelling reason and the necessary resources to lead global non-proliferation efforts. I believe that US leadership is absolutely essential to success.

There is no valid reason for future congresses or administrations to give up defending this enduring American interest. For the sake of future generations, it would be unforgivable to neglect any reasonable action that can help prevent nuclear proliferation, as the Test Ban Treaty clearly would. . . .

Preventing the spread of nuclear weapons demands coordinated actions based on common principles by many nations over many years. Our closest allies see the Test Ban Treaty as something they have fought for alongside the United States since the days of President Eisenhower. All other NATO members, Japan, South Korea. and most of our other security partners have ratified it. Once we ratify the Test Ban Treaty, which the rest of the world views as vital for non-proliferation, we will be better able to enlist cooperation on export controls, economic sanctions, and other coordinated responses to specific problems. (From General Shalkashvili's report to the president on the Comprehensive Test Ban Treaty, January 4, 2001.)

The entry into force of the CTBT would be a step back from the brink of disaster. Senators, of course, need to be convinced of this in terms of US national security, and the case must depend on verification as well as the safety and reliability of the US nuclear stockpile. The fact is that the ability to verify compliance has been strengthened immensely in the last several years, and the safety and reliability of US nuclear weapons remain certified through the Stockpile Stewardship and Management Program and those who carry it out.

Nuclear uncertainties and risks have grown since 1996 not because a test ban treaty is in place but because it is not. The risks come in the form of five nuclear weapons tests, as of 2016, by North Korea, nuclear saber-rattling in Russia, uncertainties regarding the sustainability of the Iran agreement, and an incipient nuclear arms race in South Asia. Nuclear terrorism is a potential threat to all the world's great cities. The nonproliferation regime is under serious pressure and badly needs the reinforcement that entry into force of the test ban treaty could provide.

By establishing a legally binding test ban that includes an already well-functioning International Monitoring System, which would be supplemented by on-site inspections, nuclear arms competition and nuclear proliferation would be restrained. China's ratification of the treaty, accompanied by regional security cooperation in Northeast Asia, also could deliver much-needed additional pressure on leaders in Pyongyang to join the international nuclear test moratorium and the test ban treaty itself.

Could the moratorium arrangements be strengthened pending ratification of the treaty? They could be. Transparency at national nuclear test sites would be one way. Another would be clarification of the understandings about what is permitted and not permitted in terms of explosive tests involving nuclear materials under voluntary, unilateral moratoriums. Cooperative exchanges of information also would strengthen the moratorium regime.

Such commitments as these could be reduced to writing. A nuclear test explosion, for example, might be defined as any explosive event leading to a self-sustaining nuclear chain reaction. The readiness of the parties to accept certain types of sensors at their test sites and to exchange information might be included in order to strengthen the ability to verify compliance. It would be a simple agreement that would not be difficult to negotiate, given the political will. Appendix C contains an illustrative text.

These steps would, at a minimum, add to the stability of the moratorium regime. They might also reassure those critics who object to the test ban treaty because they see in it no definition of a nuclear explosion. To be clear, a strengthened test moratorium, though a contribution to strategic stability, is not a substitute for a ratified test ban treaty.

THE IMPORTANCE OF MOMENTUM

Any of the measures identified in the agenda laid out in this chapter would have two benefits: one is that the world would be a safer place; the other is that momentum would be imparted to a process of engagement and negotiation that is now almost completely absent from the global and regional stages. Momentum is acutely important, even though largely a matter of psychology, because in the absence of some ongoing, successful process, complacency and fatalism set in, followed quickly by the disappearance of any vision of a better future for humanity. This is where we are now, in 2017. And, as President Kennedy once quoted from Proverbs 29:18 "Where there is no vision, the people perish."

NOTES

1. The following discussion is adapted from an article I wrote for the *Foreign Service Journal*. It appeared in the November 2014 issue under the title "The Putin

Doctrine and Preventive Diplomacy," http://www.afsa.org/putin-doctrine-and-preventive-diplomacy-need-consensus-american-goals.

2. "Gardening" is how Secretary of State George P. Shultz and George Kennan have described the work of staying in close touch with other nations in order to nip potential problems in the bud.

3. James Goodby, "Commonwealth and Concert: Organizing Principles of Post-Containment Order in Europe," *The Washington Quarterly* 14, no. 3 (Summer 1991).

4. James Goodby, "A Stable Peace in Europe: Can the Continent Put War Behind It?" *Brookings Review* (Summer 1999).

5. Wolfgang Ischinger, Igor Ivanov, and Sam Nunn, *International Herald Tribune* (January 31, 2012).

6. "Joint Comprehensive Plan of Action," *US Department of State*, https://www.state.gov/e/eb/tfs/spi/iran/jcpoa/.

7. Timothy L. Savage, "China's Policy Towards North Korea," *International Journal on World Peace* 20, no. 3 (2007).

8. James Goodby, "Transparency in the Middle East," *Arms Control Today* XXI, no. 4 (May 1991).

9. "History," *Nuclear Security Summit*, http://www.nss2016.org/.

10. "Joint Comprehensive Plan of Action," *US Department of State*, https://www.state.gov/e/eb/tfs/spi/iran/jcpoa/.

11. See also *The War That Must Never Be Fought: Dilemmas of Nuclear Deterrence*, eds. George P. Shultz and James E. Goodby (Stanford, CA: Hoover Institution Press, 2015). See particularly chapter 15 by James Goodby and Steven Pifer.

12. "Taking Forward Multilateral Nuclear Disarmament Negotiations," *The United Nations Office at Geneva*, http://www.unog.ch/oewg-ndn.

13. "Full Voting Result on UN Resolution L.41," *International Campaign to Abolish Nuclear Weapons*, http://www.icanw.org/campaign-news/results/.

14. See endnote 42 of chapter 4.

15. "Nuclear Deterrence and the Alliance in the 21st Century," *NATO Review*, http://www.nato.int/docu/Review/2016/Also-in-2016/nuclear-deterrence-alliance-21st-century-nato/EN/index.htm.

16. "Clinton Issues Pledge to NPT Non-Nuclear Weapon States," *Federation of American Scientists*, https://fas.org/nuke/control/npt/docs/940405-nsa.htm. "Reaction to Nuclear Powers' Assurances to NPT Parties," *Federation of American Scientists*, https://fas.org/nuke/control/npt/news/950414-387419.htm.

17. John Shalikashvili, "Shalikashvili CTBT Report: Findings and Recommendations Concerning the Comprehensive Nuclear Test Ban Treaty," *The Acronym Institute for Disarmament Diplomacy* 53 (December 2000/January 2001), http://www.acronym.org.uk/old/archive/dd/dd53/53shal.htm.

Six

Choosing the Future

> There is nothing more difficult to take in hand, more perilous to conduct, or more uncertain in its success, than to take the lead in the introduction of a new order of things.
>
> —Niccolò Machiavelli

The historical era that forms the basis for most of the story this book is telling is relatively brief, only from 1939 through 2016, well short of a century. Yet the changes in humanity's condition during that time have been so sweeping and so fundamental that Alvin Toffler's use of the term *future shock* to describe the impact on people nearly everywhere is entirely apt and may in fact be an understatement. Probably no century in human history has seen such major changes in the human condition as the period covered in this book.

For the next few decades, this will be the overwhelming reality for leaders everywhere because there is no reason to think that the pace of change will slow, despite resistance to it in many parts of the world. Integrated national policies must be put in place because single-issue policy analysis cannot serve to solve problems, and will only exacerbate them. The nuclear threat to civilization is likely to be successfully managed only in the context of an international order that prizes cooperation. Therefore, focusing only on nuclear constraints will not move the world to a safer place.

The future of humanity has always been unpredictable, but now it appears that managing the destiny of the world's peoples, or even having a major effect on the future, is an unprecedented challenge with few, if any, guideposts. As we have seen, global economic integration, with resulting changes in the international system, is one of the reasons for the growing complexity of governance. Technology is another and probably more powerful influence, both in its effect on the labor-capital balance and in its effect on national and international systems of governance.

107

GOVERNANCE IN THE DIGITAL AGE

Technology has been the main driver of change in the twenty-first century and it is likely to remain so. Its impact on society has exceeded humanity's ability to control it. In America today, children are seriously disadvantaged if they lack the means to have access to the Internet. The Internet has become a primary provider of news through social media.

Democracies are becoming more difficult to govern because the premises of their governments' legitimacy have been undermined. Most democratic nations are administered by men and women elected to represent the interests of their constituencies and to use their best judgment in doing so. Elected representatives usually try to balance local concerns with the interests of their nation as a whole. In democracies, the public has traditionally been informed by a free press that is able to criticize the government and offer alternative views about national policies. Political parties develop and publicize programs that offer alternatives for public consideration. National leaders have been chosen by the electorate in free and fair elections dominated by political parties and their adherents. The US Constitution enshrined something like this process, except for the idea of parties, which the Founders feared could lead to factionalism.

Today, most of the assumptions about how democracies work have become irrelevant to how things really work. The empowerment of every citizen, through access to social media and to information available on the Internet, has become a reality in daily life through most of the world. This empowerment has contributed significantly to a public conversation about personalities and public policy. Unfortunately, this system has been shown to be vulnerable to misuse and to deliberate manipulation.

Elected representatives often are depicted as part of an illegitimate elite that is running a government without reference to the will of the governed. Political leaders are regularly denounced on social media and blogs as either corrupt or participants in conspiracies aimed against the people. The free press, once touted in the United States as the "fourth branch of government," has been superseded by the Internet as the main source of news for large numbers of people. Many editors, reporters, and opinion leaders have fallen victim to a technology that has been exploited by those who often promote a Hobbesian view of humanity at the expense of confidence in a government of laws and a press that can be trusted to verify what it reports.

All of this has made the practice of representative democracy in the United States a very different exercise from that envisioned by the Founders, and similar developments are happening in many nations. A sign of the times came from Iceland in October 2016 when the leader of the Pirate Party called for crowdsourcing as a method of drafting a new constitution for the nation.[1] There actually is the germ of a good idea here. Representative democracy will have to develop more effective means than now exists to consult with the electorate, and it must be a two-way street—a dialogue between leaders and the public.

The authoritarian states—Russia and China in particular—have faced similar public empowerment problems. They have dealt with the challenge to central authority by controlling the media so that the government's message is loud and clear on all issues of the day, and differing opinions or sources of news can be suppressed. Authoritarian governments negotiate with Internet servers to censor their messages and they intimidate users of social media. Nationalism has been exploited to rally support for the government and to discredit independent voices, including those in organized civil society. Russia seems to have exploited social media and the Internet, using "trolls" to plant disinformation and the seeds of doubt in the minds of the citizens of other countries.[2] According to American intelligence agencies, Russian hackers broke into the computers of Americans in senior positions, and the Russian government used the data it gathered to discredit American political institutions.[3] It should surprise no one that a shadow war in cyberspace is under way. It will probably escalate in the years ahead.

This is a dangerous game in a period of heightened tensions, when hundreds of nuclear-armed missiles are ready to launch on very short notice and terrorist organizations or rogue states with their own agendas also have cyberwar capabilities. Because of cyber capabilities that are now available in sophisticated form to nations and to private organizations, nuclear confrontations are now even more potentially dangerous than during the Cold War. In a sense, cyber capabilities have become the "great equalizer" that nuclear weapons were thought to be in earlier decades. Small nations can engage in cyberwar against large nations quite effectively with little concern about retaliation.

GLOBAL INTEGRATION AND ITS FAILURES

In his State of the Union Address on January 27, 2000, President Bill Clinton said, "Globalization is the central reality of our time."[4] He may have exaggerated the centrality of global economic integration then, but not by much. Working hand in glove with technology, globalization has had a profound effect on the world's population.

But in the 2016 US presidential election campaign, opposition to trade agreements won votes in regions where jobs have vanished either because US corporations have built factories where labor costs are cheaper or because US comparative advantages have shifted to a service and information economy and away from manufacturing.[5]

In his last speech to the UN General Assembly on September 20, 2016, President Obama cited the positive features of global economic integration:

> The integration of our global economy has made life better for billions of men, women, and children. Over the last 25 years, the number of people living in extreme poverty has been cut from nearly 40 percent of humanity to under 10 percent. That's unprecedented.[6]

Not long after that speech was delivered, the 2016 US presidential election set the stage for a serious review of the terms of international trade agreements, and even of the advantages of trade itself. Immigration policies also have come under sharp and sustained questioning. The rise of populist parties across Europe, as well as the Brexit result, show that the impact on workers displaced by the shift of industries to low-wage countries and the images of multitudes of immigrants crossing borders—seemingly almost uncontrollably—have become issues that must be addressed urgently in Europe, as in America, lest they block the ability of governments to work cooperatively with other governments to counter, among other things, existential threats to humanity.

Anne Applebaum, writing in the November 4, 2016, issue of *The Washington Post*, described the loose alliance of populist-nationalist parties in the United States and Europe, as the "Populist International" and noted that they are eager to destroy institutions, including international alliances.[7] The basic reasons for the backlash have been long since recognized:

- The threatened loss of a shared identity and a perceived threat from "the other,"
- Resistance to a governance perceived to be both alien and unsympathetic to local concerns,
- An uneven distribution of economic benefits within and between nations.

These grievances are fodder for the Internet, and the empowerment of people by the Internet affords the possibility for creating mass movements. Realizing this, the Chinese and Russian governments have joined the global economic system but reject the parts of it that undercut authoritarian rule, like its openness. They resent cultural penetration and try to resist it. Yet like most of the world, they see international trade as beneficial to their interest in enhancing the power of the state and they find it difficult to contain the communications revolution.

In Europe, the existence of the European Union diverts public resentments away from globalization and provides a lightning rod to attract grievances that otherwise would be directed at globalization and technological changes. Britain's politicians speak of "Global Britain" as the alternative to membership in the European Union, by which they mean bilateral trade agreements and little or no migration. EU citizens are allowed to move freely from one member state to another, and this has generated public resistance to EU policies.[8] Large-scale migration of people fleeing war or poverty in Africa and the Middle East has generated even more hostility to international cooperation.

The migration that has occurred so far is only a foretaste of the mass migration that will inevitably occur if humanity cannot overcome its differences in order to cooperate in reducing or adapting to climate change. The backlash to globalization and technological change has placed major obstacles in the way of cooperation to reduce existential threats. What is necessary is a responsible course correction that preserves the advantages of trade, while recognizing that capital and labor have different interests in globalization that need to be fairly reconciled.

Lawrence Summers presented a perspective on this in the *Washington Post* on July 10, 2016, when he called for "responsible nationalism," which meant that "the content of international agreements would be judged not by how much is harmonized or by how many barriers to global commerce are torn down, but by whether people as workers, consumers, and voters are empowered."[9] In discussing what this implied, Dr. Summers mentioned "a proper system of international coordination that identified capital income and prevented a race to the bottom in its taxation." The French economist Thomas Piketty has supported taxes on capital income as a method of reducing inequality.[10]

There also is a need for responsible globalization. The financial and political institutions that have been created to encourage free trade and promote global cooperation have often been blind to the plight of citizens whose lives have been severely disrupted by actions encouraged or managed by these institutions. These disruptions have to be recognized and dealt with by decision makers in those institutions, not just accepted as a necessary byproduct of an economic growth engine. Job retraining has not been an adequate response for older people.

A model that is worth considering in this regard is the US Federal Reserve System. In legislation that guides the operations of the Federal Reserve Board, the governors of the system were told not only to manage inflation but also to promote "full employment."[11] These goals often are in conflict with each other, but the Board respects its mandate and generally does everything it responsibly can to achieve low inflation and high employment.

ASSESSING THE IMPACT

Which will have the greater impact over the next few decades, global integration or technology? There is no doubt that technology will dwarf global economic integration in its effect on human society, partly because technology is making global economic integration less attractive than it once was. Science and technology are likely to continue their tasks of creation, with few impediments and quite a lot of support in most advanced societies. In contrast, the process of global integration, which encourages "creative destruction," already has serious opponents. The losers in the globalization process can and do wield political power, enhanced by the impact of social media. That will continue. If the mobility of populations is not an option, often the case in the United States, large pockets of poverty and despair may persist through generations. Recently, influential books have graphically described the result.[12]

The more powerful pushback against global integration will come from technology. As T. X. Hammes of the US National Defense University, has pointed out, with labor costs of production declining to a small fraction of overall costs because of the impact of technology, incentives to locate production facilities in countries with low-cost labor will be significantly reduced.[13] Other incentives will become more important, such as proximity to markets, pressures on companies to locate their facilities in their home countries, taxes, and transportation costs. Comparative advantages in production are not limited to labor costs, so some incentives to offshoring production will remain. But for labor cost reasons, offshoring factories probably will not be as important a factor as it is today.

In the interim, there are short-term, well-understood national policies available in the United States and elsewhere to reduce the negative effects of global integration, but governments have to be able and willing to take them. For example, in an October 2016 article in *Politico*, Nelson Cunningham lists several actions, including expanding the Trade Adjustment Assistance Act, to train more workers and to help communities devastated by plant closings. A meaningful wage insurance program, one that would fill the gap between pay received from old jobs and those received from new ones, also could be useful.[14]

Any of these recommendations about softening the blows of job losses due to global integration would be difficult politically and, over the long run, may not be necessary if technology reduces the labor-cost incentives for offshoring production centers. The impact of job losses caused by robots replacing workers and the potential for income inequality caused by the empowerment of capital at the expense of labor may still require offsetting public policies.

Thomas Piketty analyzed income inequality in historical experience in his book *Capitalism in the Twenty-First Century*.[15] He wrote that in the 1910s and 1920s in the United States, the top decile of the population received 45 to 50 percent of national income. This dipped to 30 to 35 percent by the end of the 1940s and remained there in the 1950s through the 1970s. Inequality began to rise again in the 1980s, and by 2000 the top decile was back to 45 to 50 percent of national income.

Piketty acknowledged that technology will have some effect on the distribution of income in the twenty-first century, as it has in the past, but he tended to think its impact on economies will not change very much as compared with previous historic experience. Arguably, he may have underestimated the effects of artificial intelligence and robotics; if so, the balance of income could shift more strongly to the top decile.

ADAPTING TO ROBOTICS AND ARTIFICIAL INTELLIGENCE

It is not yet clear what the impact of these technologies will be, beyond the certainty that human labor will have to adjust to new realities. Experience in previous technological revolutions suggests that using new technologies in industries has created new jobs, not simply destroyed old ones. So the "creative destruction" engineered by capitalism, this time manifested in robotics and artificial intelligence, may create new and better jobs even as it destroys older means of production. Is it possible that this more cheerful assessment of the future means that the capital-labor balance of the robotics–artificial intelligence world will not materially influence the distribution of wealth? Because of demographics, that may well be the case.

Writing in *The Washington Post* on December 4, 2016, Ruchir Sharma argued that "population trends are the most powerful force shaping the rise and fall of nations."[16] There will be "declines in the working age population" in some advanced nations and robots will have to make up for a labor shortage. Moreover, job growth, Sharma says, has been relatively strong in the major industrial countries since 2008. If robots had already been replacing human workers, job growth should not be so strong. This view implies that labor will continue to hold its own in wealth distribution but it may not hold true if the use of robotics and artificial intelligence accelerates.

There are other important technological developments that may enable the movement of jobs into smaller, local production sites that could provide work for many more people than the present system of megaproduction offers. In this scenario, with relative labor costs less of a factor than at present, production could be decentralized as new means of efficient production become available to smaller units. This would be a small business-dominated world, a return to the cottage industries of the preindustrial revolution era.

Thomas Jefferson thought that democracy would be best served by decentralized, local entities. The potential of globalization to benefit humanity is huge, but new ways of dealing with change are needed and policies promoting decentralization, a concept well known to development specialists, should be considered.

The following assessment made by the UN Development Programme (UNDP) in February 1998 suggests the possible consequences of a well-conceived decentralization program. If supported by technologies that should be available in the near future, decentralization might be a useful strategy in the United States, which needs more emphasis in public policy.

> Decentralization is a counterpoint to globalization. Globalization often removes decisions from the local and national stage to the global sphere of multi-national or non-national interests. Decentralization on the other hand brings decision-making back to the sub-national and local levels. In designing decentralization strategies, it is necessary to view the interrelations of these various dimensions—global, regional, national, sub-national, local. In this regard, the role of the nation-state gains increased importance as a mediating force between the forces of globalization and localization.[17]

Digital fabrication has been described as the means by which "anyone can make anything, anywhere."[18] As the logical expansion of 3-D printing, large-scale application is probably still years away, but it offers one vision of how decentralized production might work in the future. Whether its promise will be fully realized is uncertain, but something like this means of production could support localized production of goods and services. Distributed energy production should be pursued, in any case, for national security reasons. The US national grid is vulnerable to sabotage and natural events.

Technology undoubtedly has more surprises in store for us, but one thing is clear already: a policy focus on rolling back trade and global integration would be misplaced. The effects on labor that are caused by technology already are being felt and will only be magnified in the next decade. Radical thinking about this situation is in order and leadership equal to the challenge will be necessary on an international, as well as a regional and global, basis.

It is tempting to think that powerful nations could weather this ongoing economic storm in isolation from regional and global integration of some kind. Democracies might indeed fare better than highly centralized authoritarian states because of their openness to outside influences and innovation. But technology is driving the emergence of a new, still little-understood global system, and national governments will have to think more together about how to guide and shape change, not just resist it by turning inward. A new global system can serve national purposes only if it is constructed as a joint enterprise, broadly based and broadly conceived. That method also will produce maximum benefits for humanity.

THE NUCLEAR IMPERATIVE

Such a time as humanity is now living through is perhaps without precedent, but the period after World War II showed that international institutions can assist in the transition to a different world. That lesson is now being questioned. It is true that new challenges are not being well met by existing institutions. There is no doubt that the most immediate threat to humanity—to its very survival, not to mention humanity's safe transition to a world enriched by all the good things that technology can bring—is the possibility of a nuclear war. Today, as for the past several decades, we all live in a world where a nuclear holocaust could be only an hour away. It is amazing that we have become so comfortable with a situation that earlier generations thought intolerable—"a horrible epoch," in Winston Churchill's words.

President Obama spoke at Hiroshima on May 27, 2016, in a way that sums up a central message of this book. He said:

Technological progress without an equivalent progress in human institutions can doom us. The scientific revolution that led to the splitting of an atom requires a moral revolution as well.

And he remarked that,

Among those nations like my own that hold nuclear stockpiles, we must have the courage to escape the logic of fear and pursue a world without them. . . .

We must change our mind-set about war itself. . . . And perhaps above all, we must reimagine our connection to one another as members of one human race.

The president concluded with these words:

That is a future we can choose, a future in which Hiroshima and Nagasaki are known not as the dawn of atomic warfare but as the start of our own moral awakening.[19]

To say that nuclear weapons cannot be uninvented is a truism. But the *physical nature* of the nuclear instruments that exercise a deterrent or dissuasive effect can take many forms. Deterrence is in the eye of the beholder. That has been true throughout the history of the nuclear age. The nuclear *means* chosen by governments to achieve the desired effect of inducing caution in an opponent's calculations have been surprisingly fluid and, in historical terms, even volatile. Dwight Eisenhower thought that a hundred nuclear weapons, more or less, might suffice to deter the Soviet Union he knew from invading Western Europe. His successor, John Kennedy, thought that it would take over a thousand. These numbers were not primarily a reflection of changing Soviet military strength or policies but, rather, of doctrinal changes in American thinking.

Jimmy Carter approved a strategy he called "protracted nuclear war."[20] His successor, Ronald Reagan, adopted a policy of radical reductions in nuclear weapons that, in effect, reversed the doctrine of protracted nuclear war. There was a change in the political leadership of the Soviet Union during Reagan's time that offered an opening for more imaginative thinking. But the numbers of Soviet weapons had been increasing at the time Reagan made his policy decisions and Soviet plans had called for further increases. The changed American attitude toward nuclear deterrence in the 1980s came about because Ronald Reagan thought that "a nuclear war could not be won and must never be fought."[21] He and his secretary of state, George Shultz, believed that the Soviet Union could change and acted on that belief. And so it did, bearing out George Kennan's prediction four decades earlier.

The consequences of using nuclear weapons in war are physical— massive destruction locally and environmental disasters globally. The consequences are also humanitarian—mass casualties with few means of medical help. This potentially leaves a disconnect between the planning— based on political considerations—and the outcomes. So, not surprisingly, the determination of what specific force structures equal an effective nuclear deterrence is defined, and always has been, by political calculations, despite Secretary of Defense McNamara's efforts during the Kennedy administration to quantify an answer to the question, "How much is enough?"

It is time for another change in the calculations about nuclear deterrence because at both the global level and the regional level, politicians and planners are mired in concepts about nuclear deterrence developed in the US-Soviet context during the height of the Cold War competition. There is no empirical basis for these concepts since there has never been a two-sided nuclear war. The question of how to eliminate nuclear weapons should long since have been the subject of serious international study and debate. The commitments (for example, NPT) already made by governments to a world without these weapons should have demanded serious and meticulous analysis. There are formidable technical obstacles to overcome but the most challenging issues are political.

A vision, like that of a world without nuclear weapons, is useful precisely because it forces us to think hard about crucial issues. For example, the caution imposed during the Cold War by nuclear weapons loaded on missiles ready to fire can conceivably be replaced in these quite different times by a nuclear infrastructure that is ready to reconstitute a nuclear arsenal, if needed. This is not a new idea but it has not received the detailed, high-level review it deserves. Now is the time for it because, as has been pointed out more than once in this book, cyber warfare and the spread of nuclear-weapons technology have magnified the risks inherent in reliance on nuclear-armed deterrence. In addition, if nations that possess nuclear weapons are willing to reduce to zero nuclear weapons, they almost certainly will insist on preserving the infrastructure for reconstituting a nuclear arsenal.

Another example of an urgently needed policy study was highlighted by the apparent violation of the treaty on Intermediate-Range Nuclear Forces (INF) by Russia in 2016. That treaty is in serious jeopardy now while nations in the Middle East, South Asia, and Northeast Asia have been developing and testing ballistic and cruise missiles. Many of these can be used for delivering nuclear warheads.

The nations of the world do not have, and badly need, agreements imposing quantitative and qualitative limits on the means of delivering nuclear warheads. The absence of such provisions has shifted the nuclear arms race to an effort to gain advantage in terms of how explosive devices are delivered to their targets.

Each of the permanent members of the Security Council and others are engaged in this exercise. The United States is expected to spend $1 trillion over the next thirty years to improve its strategic delivery systems.[22] This policy is not congruent with the need to engage in urgent negotiations about the very nature of the international system and how it can head off existential challenges to humanity's survival.

NUCLEAR WEAPONS AND THE
INTERNATIONAL SYSTEM

Hedley Bull published an essay in 1976 in which he pointed out that the control of nuclear weapons really is about defining world order.[23] Global as well as regional efforts to contain the growing threat of the missile and nuclear arms races are needed to contain the growing menace. Yet nothing is under way in either area as of this writing except for the UN-mandated effort to negotiate a treaty that would "prohibit" nuclear weapons. The outlook for humanity's ability to turn back the threat to all human life posed by nuclear weapons does not look promising. Perhaps we would be more successful if this goal became part of efforts to shape a new international system, one that would include organizational tools to manage existential threats. This is a priority and it needs to take precedence over other problems that occupy so much of the time of senior decision makers. If the nations cannot roll back the most immediate global threat that faces them within the context of an emerging international system, then their efforts to meet other challenges are likely to fail.

Despite the current unraveling of the nuclear constraint regime built over decades—in fact, because of it—the resumption of US-Russian joint efforts to deal with the nuclear threat has become an urgent matter. There is considerable room, and much need, for serious and productive negotiations between Russia and the United States. Other nations also share responsibilities for creating a peaceful international order and they should waste no time in negotiating their own commitments in parallel with or ahead of US-Russia agreements. These efforts should be complementary, not competitive. Cooperative security at the global level would buttress efforts at regional levels, and settlements of regional disputes would set good examples for large and small nations alike. This is one issue where a race to the bottom would be in everyone's interest.

The Iran nuclear agreement shows that even tough problems can be resolved but also that constant efforts are necessary to keep the nuclear trajectory in the direction of restraint. An agreement in Northeast Asia is more conceivable than most people assume, if sustained high-level attention is devoted to it. India and Pakistan may be moving fitfully to a better place in their mutual relationship. China is a question mark, but its nuclear-weapons program has been relatively modest in comparison with the programs of other nuclear-weapon states.

And again, where is the leadership to come from? That is clearly the basic question. If the United States recovers from its polarized and paralyzed governance crisis, the answer would be clear. If it does not, champions who could turn back the ominous approach of nuclear devastation will be hard to find, but we can hope that the recognition of impending disaster may help nations rise to the occasion.

IS ELIMINATION OF NUCLEAR ARSENALS A REALISTIC PROPOSITION?

Appendix B provides an expanded discussion of this question. It is drawn from *A World Without Nuclear Weapons: End-State Issues*, a book I wrote jointly with the late professor Sidney Drell in which we presented our views on key issues nations would face as they reduced their stockpiles of nuclear weapons.

Nuclear technology stands as a key example of modern technologies such as biotechnology, information technologies, and many others that are being developed at spectacular and increasingly rapid rates. These technologies can be enormously helpful, but they can overwhelm humanity if we succumb to their misuse. The nuclear threat is a more obvious and immediate example of technology that humanity must learn to control lest its enormous power be used for massive destruction. One of the themes of this book is that the most important and urgent step that national governments must take in the name of survival is to jointly shape the new international system that is now emerging so that the potential use of nuclear weapons is drastically reduced and the nuclear threat eventually eliminated. Yet, nuclear weapons are not even listed among the top ten concerns identified by Americans.[24]

The premise of Shultz, Kissinger, Perry, and Nunn when they began their series of appeals in 2007 for serious attention to the nuclear threat was that the goal of a world free of nuclear weapons would provide a political motivation to nations to accept a series of restraints that would move the world, step by step, toward the total elimination of nuclear weapons. From the beginning, they stressed that the world is full of complications and that regional conflicts would have to be overcome. They emphasized that a world without nuclear weapons would not be the world as it is, minus nuclear weapons. They also observed that deterrence based on nuclear weapons is becoming less effective and more dangerous.

So the first political question is whether nuclear deterrence can be abandoned. Is it still so necessary in the eyes of those nations that possess nuclear weapons that a world without them is unthinkable? Political and military leaders in the United States—Ronald Reagan first and foremost—have ventured closer to the frontier of the post-nuclear era than the leaders of many other nations have, and began that mental adjustment even before the end of the Cold War. But there is still a broadly shared faith in the United States, as elsewhere, that nuclear deterrence brings safety.

A basic question to ask about deterrence is whether it is possible for a nation to "prevail" in a nuclear war. To begin with, can damage to urban centers and massive loss of life be prevented by a counterforce strategy, that is, targeting only military installations like missile silos? It is very unlikely, given the colocation of key military targets in urban centers and considering the radiation, fires, and damage to the environment that inevitably accompany nuclear explosions. Attacks on military installations, command centers, and other prospective targets of any counterforce strategy almost inevitably imply mass civilian casualties in nearby areas. Limited or managed nuclear conflict has been studied for decades. But despite these years of effort to rationalize the use of nuclear weapons, their use is still unthinkable. As President Reagan said, their existence is justified only by the possibility that the threat of their use will prevent their use.[25]

Conceivably, the predominance of nuclear weapons as the decisive weapons of modern times is ending. The world has moved on to new generations of weaponry, such as cyber warfare and drones, which target very specific people or objects and are broadly available to almost all nations. The "ultimate weapon" may be receding into the realm of the truly unthinkable, not as Herman Kahn defined it—too horrible to contemplate—but as something so boring as to be forgettable. This would be a dangerous development if it happens because it promotes complacency, and that would be truly fatal in an era when cyber warfare could deceive governments into believing a nuclear attack is under way.

OBSTACLES TO OVERCOME

If misplaced convictions about the beneficial effects of nuclear weapons are the main obstacle to overcoming this threat to the survival of humanity, failure to resolve long-standing disputes between nations is a close second. As we saw in chapter 4, "frozen conflicts" are a major barrier to security cooperation, including the creation of conditions for a world without nuclear weapons as part of the new international system now taking shape.

The number of nuclear weapons around the world was at its peak in 1986.[26] That was the year President Reagan and Soviet General Secretary Gorbachev met at Reykjavik for one of the most consequential meetings ever held between Soviet and American leaders. The agreements they reached there led later to agreements on two major nuclear reduction treaties—on intermediate-range nuclear forces[27] and on strategic arms reductions.[28] Their discussions about eliminating nuclear weapons and relying on non-nuclear defenses broke new ground in the nuclear age. Their willingness to seriously discuss such taboo matters as ridding the world of nuclear weapons legitimized the idea for their successors. It also made it easier for Moscow and Washington to move to a less confrontational relationship, to end the division of Germany and of Europe, and, in a few short years, to end the Cold War.

This experience suggests that insulating nuclear negotiations from disruptive political events should be possible. All was not smooth sailing in US-Soviet relations during Reagan's time in office. Determined leadership by the major nations, both those that have nuclear weapons and those that do not, will be required to move out of the current impasse. It will take a considerable buildup of political momentum behind nuclear-restraint agreements in order for leaders to achieve sustainable progress in escaping the nuclear deterrence trap.

It was argued in chapter 4 that disputes are more difficult to resolve when nuclear weapons are a major factor in a bilateral relationship. This process of reducing the nuclear threat element will necessarily be a part of any successful effort to reach political settlements between rival nations in the Middle East, South Asia, or Northeast Asia. The same process will have to be resumed between Moscow and Washington and started between the United States and China. The initial effort to eliminate nuclear threats from the bilateral US-Soviet relationship launched by Reagan and Shultz began to break down in the Clinton administration with the expansion of NATO and its engagement in the former Yugoslavia. It deteriorated further during the George W. Bush administration with a US strategy of unilateralism in world affairs, including the US withdrawal from the US–Soviet Anti-Ballistic Missile Treaty and the invasion of Iraq, and reached a point of near–Cold War tension during the Obama administration over whether Ukraine would tilt East or West and with Putin's annexation of Crimea. All of this, plus ill-advised US ballistic missile defense deployments in Europe and in Korea, has made it impossible to move beyond the New START treaty that entered into force in 2011.

Similarly, disputes between Israel and its neighbors, between India and Pakistan, and between North Korea, on the one hand, and South Korea and the United States, on the other, remain unresolved after decades of hostility. The injection of nuclear weapons into the equation, as noted earlier, is both a cause and an effect: hostilities generate a demand for a nuclear deterrent, and a nuclear deterrent makes hostilities both more intense and less resolvable.

WHAT SHOULD BE DONE NOW?

The approach to a nuclear tipping point, both globally and regionally, demands that a greater sense of urgency be imparted to the effort to control nuclear weapons than is now the case. A global joint enterprise among nations is badly needed and should be organized without any further delay.[29] If a consensus could be reached among a group of leading nations that an effort should be made to eliminate nuclear weapons, they would need to establish a forum managed directly by the leaders of those nations. Institutions are essential for any long-term effort to build a new global order. Experience with forums at lower levels of governance has shown that leaders tend to lose interest in them, with the result that stale-mates and public posturing come to dominate the agenda. The Nuclear Security Summits organized by President Obama during his terms of office could be a model for an effort to eliminate nuclear weapons, but there are other possibilities, including using the UN Security Council as the core of a standing negotiating committee.

Despite the poor state of US-Russia relations, a few steps could be taken directly, and soon, with Russia. One of them would be to take land-based ballistic missiles off prompt-launch status by removing warheads. This action would be similar to the Strategic Offensive Reductions Treaty worked out by George W. Bush and Vladimir Putin.[30] Verification could be based on the New START. This would begin the process of giving Moscow and Washington more time for decisions, an important factor in light of current conditions.[31]

We also should begin to establish what Shultz, Kissinger, Perry, and Nunn have called a "Joint Enterprise," a coalition of nations willing to work together to create the conditions for a world without nuclear weapons. As mentioned above, this effort should include not only a commitment by world leaders to work together to eliminate nuclear weapons but also a mutually acceptable work program for negotiated agreements and a list of measures they are prepared to undertake right away as matters of national policy.[32] Russia and the United States should be major players in this coalition, in addition to participating in bilateral negotiations.

THE HOLY GRAIL OF ARMS CONTROL

America's real nuclear deterrent resides in the skills of its scientists and engineers more than in the numbers and types of weapons that have been manufactured at any given time. That will remain true even if all of the world's nuclear weapons have been eliminated. The George W. Bush administration advanced ideas that should be perpetuated. One of them was an emphasis on a "responsive force" that could be rapidly reconstitu-ted as a ready operational force.[33]

Because of the successes of American scientists and engineers in main-taining a safe and reliable stockpile of nuclear weapons despite the absence of any American nuclear test explosions since 1992, the United States can confidently embark on a campaign to enlist the world's pos-sessors of nuclear weapons in a long-term effort to reduce and eliminate nuclear weapons.

For this same reason, the United States can safely work for the entry into force of a comprehensive, global ban on all explosive nuclear tests. This will not be easy, for some nations will want to enjoy the freedom to test their newly designed nuclear weapons, unencumbered by a treaty banning such tests. The most threatening of those nations are not allies of the United States nor are they friends of the Nuclear Non-Proliferation Treaty. American diplomacy has had to work with one hand tied behind its back because the US Senate has not yet given its advice and consent to the ratification of a test ban treaty that still lies before it.

The test ban is an absolutely essential element in a network of barriers against proliferation—not a panacea in itself, but critical to the success of the whole project. The treaty would prevent advanced nuclear-weapon states from making significant improvements in their weapons stockpiles, and it would prevent non-nuclear-weapon states from developing more sophisticated weapons.

What the nuclear powers do affects the decisions of other countries. One would think that is a truism, but it is hotly debated. Some opponents of the test ban argue that whether the United States tests or develops new weapons has no effect on what the other nations do. But, in fact, expectations about the future are what motivate most governments and most people. Explosive testing is perhaps the most visible of all nuclear-weapon activities. A nuclear explosion amounts to an announcement that nuclear weapons are here to stay. That is what testing tells the world.

With strong leadership from Washington, Moscow, Beijing, and other key capitals, the treaty could be brought into force.[34] Otherwise, the door to additional testing and dangerous proliferation will remain open. The United States no longer has an overwhelming military or technical reason to resume nuclear testing, but nuclear testing can help other states, such as North Korea, develop small, more easily deliverable nuclear weapons. If testing resumes by any major nation, such as China or India, it could cascade into a competition that would be hard to stop.

US action on the Comprehensive Test Ban Treaty (CTBT) would make all the difference. If the United States ratified the CTBT, China's leaders would want to consider completing their delayed ratification process. Just the process of rethinking Beijing's position would place pressure on India and Pakistan. North Korea must also ratify in order for the treaty to enter into force, and a move by the bigger powers to ratify should oblige Pyongyang to consider joining in a growing consensus. Israel and Iran already have signed the treaty and, depending on conditions in the Middle East, a cascade of ratifications should influence them in a positive direction. US failure to ratify, in contrast, had a direct effect on China's thinking about nuclear issues and that encouraged India to keep its nuclear testing options open. If the Indian prime minister were convinced that entry into force of the CTBT would advance India's interests, he would probably be able to win over Indian public opinion. With the

United States, China, and India ratifying the treaty, Pakistan would certainly want to reconsider its position. This speculation about a benign cycle of events might be wishful thinking but the results of US inaction on ratification are all too predictable.[35]

A PLACE FOR BALLISTIC MISSILE DEFENSE?

Will ballistic missile defense help us out of our predicament? Here is what Ronald Reagan said about this in a letter to Gorbachev in July 1986: "I believe you would agree that significant commitments of this type with respect to strategic defenses would make sense only if made in conjunction with the implementation of immediate actions on both sides to begin moving toward our common goal of the total elimination of nuclear weapons."[36] Unfortunately, we are not moving very rapidly toward that goal. Eisenhower was skeptical of nuclear defense because of what he called the "awful arithmetic" of the atomic bomb.[37] It is cheaper and easier to add offensive weapons and decoys than to build defenses. That is still true today. The United States, Russia, and China have had serious differences of opinion about the impact of US ballistic defense systems in Europe and, potentially, in Asia. These differences have blocked efforts to cooperate in reducing the nuclear threat. A review of US policy in this area should have a high priority, and the review should discuss engaging in a cooperative missile-defense effort, which could avoid some of the pitfalls of unilateral defenses.

COOPERATIVE SECURITY REGIMES AND
PUBLIC DECISION MAKING

It is now obvious that resolving the nuclear threat to humanity requires a broader framework than is afforded by even the most ambitious agenda for nuclear restraints. This statement has been true in the case of regions for a long time, and is widely recognized. It is now apparent that this statement applies to global efforts to turn back the nuclear threat as well. The chaos besetting the international system makes it difficult for the governments of nation-states to negotiate agreements to reduce and eventually eliminate nuclear weapons. At least in parallel with, if not in advance of, efforts to eliminate the existential nuclear threat to humanity, an effort must also be made to turn back the current, and growing, threat to the ability of governments to exercise the authority necessary for the creation of cooperative security regimes. This requires some kind of organizational support. A brief excursion into regime theory will suggest what is involved in this last simple declaratory sentence.

Various definitions of an "international regime" have been offered.[38] Essentially, it is a condition in which nations are prompted to act jointly in ways that they might not act if left to their own devices. What causes such behavior or even whether it exists is debated among political scientists, but as a diplomat, I witnessed behavior among nations that bears out the thesis that governments do often act as though they were part of a "regime."[39]

Applying the general theory of international regimes to the practical question of how to go about creating such regimes, Oran R. Young postulated that "regime formation in international society ordinarily involves some form of collective action."[40] His preferred description for this action was "institutional design at the international level," by which he meant "deliberate or planned alterations in institutional arrangements in the interests of achieving identifiable goals." But Young did not conceive of regime formation as a kind of top-down imposition of a preconceived, rational plan of action. Rather, he saw it in terms of what we would today call "design thinking."[41] He wrote that it is seldom, if ever, feasible at the outset to identify a well-defined contract zone in the complex bargaining involved in negotiating the provisions of international regimes.

What this analysis implies is that classical means of negotiating should be augmented by a more bottom-up approach at some point in the process. Just as engineers trying to solve a problem engage in brainstorming, so should delegations and policy makers engage first in a freewheeling process of looking for solutions that solve common problems between nations. Probably, nations would have to engage first in Track II (informal, nongovernmental) explorations rather than in formal negotiations, but the results in terms of regime creation should eventually merit a serious effort backed by governments.

BRINGING NATIONAL DECISION
MAKING UP TO DATE

The goal of creating a cooperative security regime is inseparable from the international context in which the effort would be made. As this and previous chapters have recorded, globalization and technology have resulted in a public backlash and public repudiation of both globalization and some of the economic results of advances in technology. It is unlikely that either globalization or technology will go away, although both might be set back by public opinion. That being the case, governments need policies that will maximize the positive effects of these characteristics of our time while minimizing the negative effects.

The positive effects include broad advances in human well-being which by far outweigh negative consequences, but these advances tend to be unequally distributed and fully absorbed only over the long-term while many of the negative consequences, such as local economic disruption, are felt more immediately.

Following the precepts discussed above regarding regime creation and design thinking, a US administration operating in a context that is likely to be manifested by opposition to international cooperation must proactively work with the American public in order to achieve results. Top-down imposition of the elements of a cooperative security regime simply will not work.

A model that is more suited to present circumstances is one in which stakeholders are involved at an early stage. That notion has already been useful in garnering support for controversial construction proposals. Now it is a necessity across a spectrum of public policy issues.

What does this mean in practice? The model frequently used by the Department of Energy is to engage communities where energy installations are going to be located in discussions about the environmental and other impacts of the project. Stakeholders are identified early on and they retain a voice in decision making throughout the project.

On a much broader scale, a US administration or the Congress could do the same. For example, the president or the Congress might establish a commission, or perhaps a series of them on a regional basis, to recommend or react to proposed national policies on a specific public issue. These could include international trade agreements, communications policies, or cooperative security proposals, to cite three highly controversial subjects. The commissions could be composed of people from various walks of life. They would be empowered to invite experts, ordinary citizens, and government officials to join them in discussions on various aspects of the issue.

Other models could be more unstructured. Excellent examples of this are discussions about artificial intelligence reportedly being carried on by industry and universities. Engaging corporations and nongovernmental organizations in conversations about emerging technologies is essential. For example, as advanced by MIT, new artificial intelligence and robotic systems would be designed with "society in the loop."[42]

If this process of decision making sounds complicated, it is. But we are passing through a real revolution in public discourse, and the empowerment of citizens means that, one way or another, they are going to have an enhanced say in ongoing public decision making in order to supplement the process of representative government. The alternatives to a model something like this are: (1) a more authoritarian US government; (2) anarchy; or (3) constant sniping by disaffected groups of citizens, with the result being that decisions have to be revisited periodically.

How might such a broad-based system of citizen involvement conduct business? Here is an illustration: Chapter 3 offers six hypothetical rules regarding the operation of the Internet. Taken together, these six rules constitute an undeclared regime affecting the way people around the world act within the environment made possible by the Internet. US presidents and the Congress already are confronting the question of regulation of Internet practices in multiple areas. So under a system that involves the public more directly in decisions with major public consequences, a president or the Congress would convene a commission, or a series of commissions, charged with recommending rules of the road for operation of the Internet, perhaps based on something like the six rules cited in chapter 3, and suggesting how regulation and enforcement might work in practice. Probably some pump-priming would help, and draft commentaries on each of the six hypothetical rules could be offered by the convening authority; for example, the president, a congressional resolution, or a federal agency.

All this would be very cumbersome, but the empowerment of citizens through the information technology revolution has not been kind to our system of representative government in the United States. If we are to preserve it, we will have to augment it with a system that brings American citizens more directly into at least the early stages of national policy making in some organized and structured procedure.

Changes in decision making on major policy issues have profound implications for diplomacy. Such a system could bring transparency into a delicate negotiating process in a way that could chill the kind of informal, noncommittal explorations of ideas that are the lifeblood of negotiations. WikiLeaks may already have had that effect. On the other hand, negotiations would benefit from a process that advised diplomats in advance about the public's reaction to various options. This could make it easier to imagine adjustments in policies that would be inherent in a design-thinking approach.

At some point, the Constitution will draw the line. Representative government must assert itself or American institutions created by the Constitution would be vitiated. As has been said, "The Constitution is not a suicide pact." It can accommodate many ways to reach a national decision, but it cannot hand over decision powers to institutions or procedures that are extra-Constitutional.

The decision-making procedures described above would have special value under present circumstances in harnessing new technologies. Technology has helped to create a communications revolution that supports a globalized economy and empowers individual citizens through instant access to extended networks of people, regardless of borders. If nations manage this development well and use it to involve their publics in a considered examination of other sensitive issues, such as genetics, the benefits for humanity can be enormous. "Crowdsourcing" is not a bad idea.

THE POLITICS OF INCLUSION

In 1974, Andrei Sakharov foresaw what he called a "universal information system (UIS)." It was an amazingly accurate description of the Internet and social media as we know them today. He described how this would affect everyone and concluded that "the true historic role of the UIS will be to break down the barriers to the exchange of information among countries and people."[43]

The challenge before us lies in the struggle between open and closed societies, between nationalism that seeks to divide and nationalism that is built on universal values. One type of nationalism discourages diversity; the other type welcomes it. One type looks to the past and is inwardly focused; the other looks outward and to the future.

What does this mean for those who cherish diversity and openness? Should they draw lines between nations that encourage these characteristics and nations that try to shut down the Internet and teach intolerance toward points of view other than their own? Here, we can do no better than follow Sakharov's prescient advice, offered in 1968:[44]

> The division of mankind threatens it with destruction. Civilization is imperiled by: a universal thermonuclear war, catastrophic hunger for most of mankind, stupefaction from the narcotic of "mass culture," and bureaucratized dogmatism, a spreading of mass myths that put entire peoples and continents under the power of cruel and treacherous demagogues, and destruction or degeneration from the unforeseeable consequences of swift changes in the conditions of life on our planet.
>
> In the face of these perils, any action increasing the division of mankind, any preaching of the incompatibility of world ideologies and nations is madness and a crime.

In a nutshell, the politics of inclusion, even in the face of rejection and derision from those who seek to divide, is the only way to a lasting peace.

THE COMMON INTERESTS OF
NATIONS AND PEOPLES

The structural problem humanity faces today is that international institutions established after World War II have been weakened and new global challenges have arisen that are not being met either by nations or by international institutions. Cooperation among nations obviously has been hard to achieve. Regionalism is a potentially effective form of cooperation as the European Union has proved, despite its current difficulties, but regions are too often thought of as closed to outsiders—a way of maximizing national power, not as a contribution to a global system that would benefit humanity. At the same time, global economic integration is perceived to be inimical to the interests of ordinary citizens, and internationalism itself is under attack. New technologies are being misused to foster mass myths, as Sakharov put it, and to generate hostility among nations and peoples. The sense of uncertainty and complexity is acute, with old dangers taking new shapes and new dangers not yet well understood.

Unrestrained competition—zero-sum games—inevitably bring bad outcomes and should constitute a standing incentive for restraint. This type of thinking is increasingly prevalent and it prevents serious thinking and action on urgent global challenges, not just about nuclear deterrence but about many of our institutions and assumptions. It is a Hobbesian approach, very much out of tune with the spirit of America's founding documents, the Declaration of Independence, and the Constitution.[45]

The task of creating norms and management tools that benefit nations and ordinary citizens has to act in accordance with the bedrock fact that only through global cooperation will life or death threats to nations be rolled back. Fortunately, there is no inherent reason why the interests of local and national societies and of a global society should be mutually contradictory.

Nation-states remain the main engines for managing the global security commons, as it evolves. Coalitions of nations are struggling with global issues such as climate change but the array of security issues that confronts all humanity needs more attention. Institutions such as the United Nations, World Trade Organization (WTO), World Bank, International Monetary Fund (IMF), European Union, and North Atlantic Treaty Organization (NATO) are dealing, with varying degrees of success, with regional security issues and with the global economic commons. These institutions generally have not focused intensively on existential issues as these have arisen in recent decades but this is beginning to change.

What would it take to accelerate the capacity-building process? It is easier to say it than to do it, but certainly it would take a summit-level commitment, a determined multiyear effort with clear goals, and public acceptance that a global security commons involves life-or-death challenges that can only be met through cooperation among national governments at both the regional and the global levels.

NATIONAL SECURITY AND HOW TO ACHIEVE IT

The threat of nuclear weapons affords an opportunity to show what cooperative security can do. Years of experience have provided many lessons.

One of them is that momentum for major nuclear reductions has to be built and supported by increasingly cooperative international relationships. This was shown by the experience of the Reagan-Gorbachev revolution which also showed that US-Russian cooperation is essential to survival. The United States and its allies, with Russian counterparts, must look for ways to reduce both their respective strategic arsenals and the numbers of tactical weapons in Europe. No less energy and attention ought to be paid to the question of nuclear weapons in Asia, where the trend is toward an increasing quantity and quality of nuclear arms and delivery systems, including small tactical weapons ideal for being commandeered by terrorists. Broad summit-level commitment to the goal of managing, curbing, and eliminating nuclear arms should be accompanied by a greater emphasis on addressing regional instabilities, rivalries, and latent conflicts, which animate the drive toward nuclear arms.

What is being proposed here is a major shift in the way countries' policy makers view national security requirements in a changing international system. It is no less visionary than those ideas held by leaders in the late 1940s and 1950s who sponsored the UN, NATO, EU, and international financial organizations; these resulted in seven decades of non-war, or conditional peace, among the major powers of the world and significant economic development on a broad basis. Strategic foresight and political courage matching or exceeding those of earlier times are now needed on the part of the current and next generation of leaders. The nation-states are still the main engines of cooperation and conflict, and how they organize their affairs in the vast realm external to each individual nation-state is key to war and peace and to reducing anarchy in relations among states.

Recognizing that the task of eliminating nuclear weapons will be daunting President Obama remarked in his speech in Prague in 2009 that "fatalism is a deadly adversary."[46] Developments since then confirm his insight and the fact that fatalism in the task of responding to all challenges to humanity's survival will only lead to disaster.

Most of the great threats to the survival of civilization and perhaps of the human race are global in nature, and for reasons of resources, among others, they cannot be managed by national or limited regional responses. The challenge is for each major nation to create mechanisms to invent and support management systems that will deal with common challenges. Time is of the essence.

NOTES

1. Tara John, "Everything You Need to Know About Iceland's Pirate Party," *Time* (October 28, 2016), http://time.com/4549089/iceland-pirate-party-general -election-populist/.

2. Natasha Bertrand, "It Looks Like Russia Hired Internet Trolls to Pose as Pro-Trump Americans," *Business Insider* (July 27, 2016), http://uk.businessinsider .com/russia-internet-trolls-and-donald-trump-2016-7.

3. "The Perfect Weapon: How Russian Cyberpower Invaded the US," *The New York Times* (December 13, 2016), https://www.nytimes.com/2016/12/13/us/ politics/russia-hack-election-dnc.html?_r=0.

4. James E. Goodby, Petrus Buwalda, and Dmitri Trenin, *A Strategy for Stable Peace: Toward a Euroatlantic Security Community* (Washington, DC: United States Institute of Peace Press, 2002). For details of the State of the Union Address, see http://www.washingtonpost.com/wp-srv/politics/special/states/docs/sou00 .htm.

5. "US Election 2016: Trump Victory in Maps," *BCC News* (December 1, 2016), http://www.bbc.co.uk/news/election-us-2016-37889032.

6. "Address by President Obama to the 71st Session of the United Nations General Assembly," *The White House*, https://obamawhitehouse.archives.gov/ the-press-office/2016/09/20/address-president-obama-71st-session-united-nations -general-assembly.

7. Anne Applebaum, "Trump Is a Threat to the West As We Know It, Even if He Loses," *The Washington Post* (November 4, 2016).

8. Toby Helm, "Migration Backlash in the European Union: Year in Review 2016," *Encyclopedia Britannica* (December 14, 2016), https://www.britannica .com/topic/Migration-Backlash-in-the-European-Union-2083751.

9. Lawrence Summers, "How to Embrace Nationalism Responsibly," *The Washington Post* (July 10, 2016), https://www.washingtonpost.com/opinions/ global-opinions/how-to-embrace-nationalism-responsibly/2016/07/10/faf7a100 -4507-11e6-8856-f26de2537a9d_story.html?utm_term=.998b58d094d4.

10. Thomas Piketty, *Capitalism in the Twenty-First Century* (Cambridge, MA: The Belknap Press of the Harvard University Press, 2014).

11. "H.R.3541—Full Employment Federal Reserve Act of 2015," 114th Congress, https://www.congress.gov/bill/114th-congress/house-bill/3541/text.

12. See, for example John D. Vance, *Hillbilly Elegy: A Memoir of a Family and Culture in Crisis* (New York: HarperCollins Publishers, 2016).

13. T. X. Hammes, "Will Technological Convergence Reverse Globalization?" *Institute for National Strategic Studies, Strategic Forum* 297 (July 12, 2016), http:// inss.ndu.edu/Media/News/Article/834444/will-technological-convergence -reverse-globalization/.

14. Nelson Cunningham, "The Liberal Case for Free Trade," *Politico* (October 28, 2016), http://www.politico.com/agenda/story/2016/10/the-liberal-case-for -free-trade-000226.

15. See endnote 10 of chapter 6.

16. Ruchir Sharma, "Robots Won't Kill the Workforce. They'll Save the Economy," *The Washington Post* (December 4, 2016). Sharma is chief global strategist at Morgan Stanley Investment Management. See also Martin Ford, *Rise of the Robots: Technology and the Threat of a Jobless Future* (New York: Basic Books, 2015), who argues that more jobs will not be created and that guaranteed annual incomes will be necessary. Also see the article by Farhad Manjoo, "A Plan in Case Robots

Take the Jobs: Give Everyone a Paycheck," *The New York Times* (March 2, 2016), in which a "universal basic income" as a necessary accompaniment of the new technology is discussed. https://www.nytimes.com./2016/03/03/technology/plan-to-fight-robot-invasion-at-work-give-everyone-a-paycheck.html.

17. "Decentralization: A Sampling of Definitions," a working paper prepared in connection with the joint UNDP–Government of Germany evaluation of the UNDP role in decentralization and local governance, October 1999.

18. Neil Gershenfeld, "How to Make Almost Anything: The Digital Fabrication Revolution," *Foreign Affairs* (November/December 2012), 43–57.

19. Barack Obama, "Remarks by President Obama and Prime Minister Abe of Japan at Hiroshima Peace Memorial," *The White House*, https://obamawhite house.archives.gov/the-press-office/2016/05/27/remarks-president-obama-and-prime-minister-abe-japan-hiroshima-peace.

20. James E. Goodby, *At the Borderline of Armageddon: How American Presidents Managed the Atom Bomb* (Lanham, MD: Rowman & Littlefield Publishers, 2006).

21. Ronald Reagan, "Address Before a Joint Session of the Congress on the State of the Union January 25, 1984," http://www.presidency.ucsb.edu/ws/?pid=40205.

22. William J. Broad and David E. Sanger, "Race for Latest Class of Nuclear Arms Threatens to Revive Cold War," *The New York Times*, April 17, 2016, https://www.nytimes.com/2016/04/17/science/atom-bomb-nuclear-weapons-hgv-arms-race-russia-china.html.

23. Hedley Bull, "Arms Control and World Order," *International Security* 1, no. 1 (July 1976): 3–16.

24. "Americans' Priorities for 2017," *The Associated Press–NORC Center for Public Affairs Research*, http://www.apnorc.org/projects/Pages/HTML%20Reports/americans-priorities-for-2017-issue-brief.aspx.

25. Ronald Reagan, "Address Before a Joint Session of the Congress on the State of the Union January 25, 1984," https://reaganlibrary.archives.gov/archives/speeches/1984/12584e.htm.

26. Hans M. Kristensen and Robert S. Norris, "Status of World Nuclear Forces," *Federation of American Scientists* (February 17, 2017), https://fas.org/issues/nuclear-weapons/status-world-nuclear-forces/.

27. "Treaty Between the United States of America and the Union of Soviet Socialist Republics on the Elimination of Their Intermediate-Range and Shorter-Range Missiles (INF Treaty)," *US Department of State*, https://www.state.gov/t/avc/trty/102360.htm.

28. "Strategic Arms Reduction Treaty I (START I)," *Arms Control Association*, https://www.armscontrol.org/treaties/strategic-arms-reduction-treaty-i.

29. See Chapter 15 in George P. Shultz and James E. Goodby, eds. *The War That Must Never Be Fought*. Stanford, CA: Hoover Institution Press, 2015.

30. START I was signed by Presidents George H. W. Bush and Boris Yeltsin on January 3, 1993.

31. See "Old Wine in New Bottles" in chapter 5 for other early actions that Russia and the United States should revive as soon as possible.

32. George P. Shultz and James E. Goodby, eds., *The War That Must Never Be*

Fought: Dilemmas of Nuclear Deterrence (Stanford, CA: Hoover Institution Press, 2015), chapter 15.

33. "Nuclear Posture Review Report," *US Department of Defense*, http://archive .defense.gov/news/Jan2002/d20020109npr.pdf.

34. For a list of nations that have signed and ratified the CTBT, please see: https://www.ctbto.org/the-treaty/status-of-signature-and-ratification/.

35. See Sidney D. Drell and James E. Goodby, *The Gravest Danger : Nuclear Weapons*. Stanford, CA: Hoover Institution Press, 2003. Chapter VI contains a lengthier discussion of these issues.

36. Sidney D. Drell, George P. Shultz, Henry A. Kissinger, and Sam Nunn, *Nuclear Security: The Problems and the Road Ahead* (Stanford, CA: Hoover Institution Press, 2014).

37. Dwight D. Eisenhower, *Public Papers of the Presidents of the United States*, 1953, https://quod.lib.umich.edu/p/ppotpus?cginame=text-idx;id=navbar browselink;page=browse.

38. Arthur Stein's analysis can be found in "Coordination and Collaboration: Regimes in an Anarchic World," *International Organization* 36, no. 2 (1982): 299–324. http://www.jstor.org/stable/2706524.

39. James E. Goodby, "Preventive Diplomacy for Nuclear Nonproliferation in the Former Soviet Union," in *Opportunities Missed, Opportunities Seized: Preventive Diplomacy in the Post–Cold War World*, ed. Bruce W. Jentleson (Lanham, MD: Rowman & Littlefield, 2000).

40. The following quotations are from Oran R. Young, *International Cooperation: Building Regimes for Natural Resources and the Environment* (Ithaca, NY: Cornell University Press, 1989).

41. Tim Brown and Jocelyn Wyatt, "Design Thinking for Social Innovation," *Stanford Social Innovation Review* (Winter 2010).

42. John Markoff, "Tech Giants Gather to Devise Real Ethics for Artificial Intelligence," *New York Times* (September 2, 2016).

43. Sidney D. Drell and George P. Shultz, eds., *Andrei Sakharov: The Conscience of Humanity* (Stanford, CA: Hoover Institution Press, 2015).

44. Andrei Sakharov, "Thoughts on Progress, Peaceful Coexistence and Intellectual Freedom," May 1968, published in the *New York Times* (July 22, 1968).

45. See *The Anarchical Society*, Hedley Bull, pp. 44–49, for a comparison of Locke and Hobbes.

46. Paul Reynolds, "Assessing Obama's Nuclear Weapons Agenda," *BBC News* (April 14, 2010), http://news.bbc.co.uk/2/hi/8617687.stm.

Appendix A

Joint Statement: Strategic Stability Cooperation Initiative Between the United States of America and Russian Federation

September 6, 2000
http://www.presidency.ucsb.edu/ws/?pid = 1392

President William Jefferson Clinton of the United States of America and President Vladimir Putin of the Russian Federation met today in New York and agreed on a Strategic Stability Cooperation Initiative as a constructive basis for strengthening trust between the two sides and for further development of agreed measures to enhance strategic stability and to counter the proliferation of weapons of mass destruction, missiles and missile technologies worldwide. In furtherance of this initiative, the two Presidents approved an implementation plan developed by their experts as a basis for continuing this work.

The Strategic Stability Cooperation Initiative builds on the Presidents' agreement in their two previous meetings. The Joint Statement on Principles of Strategic Stability, adopted in Moscow on June 4, 2000, and the Joint Statement on Cooperation on Strategic Stability, adopted in Okinawa on July 21, 2000, establish a constructive basis for progress in further reducing nuclear weapons arsenals, preserving and strengthening the ABM Treaty, and confronting new challenges to international security. The United States and Russia reaffirm their commitment to the ABM Treaty as a cornerstone of strategic stability. The United States and Russia intend to implement the provisions of the START I and INF Treaties, to seek early entry into force of the START II Treaty and its related Protocol, the 1997 New York agreements on ABM issues and the Comprehensive Nuclear Test Ban Treaty, and to work towards the early realization of the 1997 Helsinki Joint Statement on Parameters on Future Reductions in Nuclear Forces. The United States and Russia also intend to seek new forms of cooperation in the area of non-proliferation of missiles and missile technologies with a view to strengthening international security and

135

maintaining strategic stability within the framework of the Strategic Stability Cooperation Initiative between our two countries.

The Strategic Stability Cooperation Initiative could include, along with expansion of existing programs, new initiatives aimed at strengthening the security of our two countries and of the entire world community and without prejudice to the security of any state.

START III Treaty and ABM Treaty. The United States and Russia have presented their approaches to the principal provisions of the START III Treaty and on ABM issues. The United States and Russia have held intensified discussions on further reductions in strategic offensive forces within the framework of a future START III Treaty and on ABM issues, with a view to initiating negotiations expeditiously, in accordance with the Moscow Joint Statement of September 2, 1998, the Cologne Joint Statement of June 20, 1999, and the Okinawa Joint Statement of July 21, 2000 by the two Presidents. They will seek to agree upon additional measures to strengthen strategic stability and confidence, and to ensure predictability in the military field.

NPT, CTBT, FMCT, BWC, and Nuclear Weapon-Free Zones. The United States and Russia reaffirm their commitment to the Treaty on the Non-Proliferation of Nuclear Weapons as the foundation of the international nuclear nonproliferation and nuclear disarmament regime.

The United States and Russia will seek to ensure early entry into force and effective implementation of the Comprehensive Nuclear Test Ban Treaty. They will continue to work to begin negotiations to conclude a Fissile Material Cutoff Treaty and to strengthen the Biological Weapons Convention. They will continue to facilitate the establishment of nuclear weapon-free zones in the world, based on voluntary agreements among states in the relevant region, consistent with the relevant 1999 Report of the United Nations Disarmament Commission, as an important avenue for efforts to prevent nuclear weapons proliferation.

Discussions of issues related to the threat of proliferation of missiles and missile technology. The United States and Russia are prepared to expand their discussions of issues related to the threat of proliferation of missiles and missile technologies. These discussions will include annual briefings based on assessments of factors and events related to ballistic and cruise missile proliferation. Annual assessments will address potential threats to international security. With a view to preventing the proliferation of missiles and weapons of mass destruction, political and diplomatic measures will be discussed and undertaken, using bilateral and multilateral mechanisms.

Cooperation in the area of Theater Missile Defense. The United States and Russia are prepared to resume and then expand cooperation in the area of Theater Missile Defense (TMD), and also to consider the possibility of involving other states, with a view to strengthening global and regional stability.

The sides will consider as specific areas of such cooperation:

- Expansion of the bilateral program of joint TMD command and staff exercises.
- Possibility of involving other states in joint TMD command and staff exercises.
- Possibility of development of methods for enhanced interaction for joint use of TMD systems.
- Joint development of concepts for possible cooperation in TMD systems.
- Possibility of reciprocal invitation of observers to actual firings of TMD systems.

Early warning information. The United States and Russia, in implementation of the Memorandum of Agreement between the United States of America and the Russian Federation on the Establishment of a Joint Center for the Exchange of Data from Early Warning Systems and Notification of Missile Launches signed in Moscow on June 4, 2000, intend to establish and put into operation in Moscow within a year the joint center for exchange of data to preclude the possibility of missile launches caused by a false missile attack warning. The Parties will also make efforts to come to an early agreement on a regime for exchanging notifications of missile launches, consistent with the statement of the Presidents at Okinawa on July 21, 2000.

Missile Non-Proliferation measures. The United States and Russia intend to strengthen the Missile Technology Control Regime. They declare their commitment to seek new avenues of cooperation with a view to limiting proliferation of missiles and missile technologies. Consistent with the July 21, 2000, Joint Statement of the Presidents at Okinawa, they will work together with other states on a new mechanism to integrate, *inter alia*, the Russian proposal for a Global Control System for Non-Proliferation of Missiles and Missile Technologies (GCS), the US proposal for a missile code of conduct, as well as the MTCR.

Confidence and transparency-building measures. Bearing in mind their obligations under the Treaty on the Non-Proliferation of Nuclear Weapons, the United States and Russia will seek to expand cooperation related to the Comprehensive Nuclear Test Ban Treaty (CTBT) to promote a mutually beneficial technical exchange that will facilitate the implementation of the CTBT after its entry into force. The United States and Russia are prepared to discuss confidence and transparency-building measures as an element of facilitating compliance with, preserving and strengthening the ABM Treaty. These measures could include: data exchanges, pre-notifications of planned events, voluntary demonstrations, participation in observations, organization of exhibitions, and strengthening the ABM Treaty compliance verification process.

The Presidents of the United States and Russia have agreed that officials from the relevant ministries and agencies will meet annually to coordinate their activities in this area, and look forward with interest to such a meeting in the near future.

The United States and Russia call upon all nations of the world to unite their efforts to strengthen strategic stability.

The President of the United States of America
The President of the Russian Federation
New York City
September 6, 2000

DECLARATION OF PRESIDENT GEORGE W. BUSH
AND PRESIDENT VLADIMIR V. PUTIN SIGNED AT
MOSCOW On MAY 24, 2002

https://www.state.gov/t/avc/trty/127129.htm#1

JOINT DECLARATION ON THE NEW
STRATEGIC RELATIONSHIP

The United States of America and the Russian Federation,

Recalling the accomplishments at the Ljubljana, Genoa, Shanghai, and Washington/Crawford Summits and the new spirit of cooperation already achieved;

Building on the November 13, 2001, Joint Statement on a New Relationship Between the United States and Russia, having embarked upon the path of new relations for the twenty-first century, and committed to developing a relationship based on friendship, cooperation, common values, trust, openness, and predictability;

Reaffirming our belief that new global challenges and threats require a qualitatively new foundation for our relationship;

Determined to work together, with other nations and with international organizations, to respond to these new challenges and threats, and thus contribute to a peaceful, prosperous, and free world and to strengthening strategic security;

Declare as follows:

A FOUNDATION FOR COOPERATION

We are achieving a new strategic relationship. The era in which the United States and Russia saw each other as an enemy or strategic threat has ended. We are partners and we will cooperate to advance stability, security, and economic integration, and to jointly counter global challenges and to help resolve regional conflicts.

To advance these objectives the United States and Russia will continue an intensive dialogue on pressing international and regional problems, both on a bilateral basis and in international fora, including in the UN Security Council, the G-8, and the OSCE. Where we have differences, we will work to resolve them in a spirit of mutual respect.

We will respect the essential values of democracy, human rights, free speech and free media, tolerance, the rule of law, and economic opportunity.

We recognize that the security, prosperity, and future hopes of our people rest on a benign security environment, the advancement of political and economic freedoms, and international cooperation.

The further development of US-Russian relations and the strengthening of mutual understanding and trust will also rest on a growing network of ties between our societies and peoples. We will support growing economic interaction between the business communities of our two countries and people-to-people and cultural contacts and exchanges.

POLITICAL COOPERATION

The United States and Russia are already acting as partners and friends in meeting the new challenges of the 21st century; affirming our Joint Statement of October 21, 2001, our countries are already allied in the global struggle against international terrorism.

The United States and Russia will continue to cooperate to support the Afghan people's efforts to transform Afghanistan into a stable, viable nation at peace with itself and its neighbors. Our cooperation, bilaterally and through the United Nations, the "Six-Plus-Two" diplomatic process, and in other multilateral fora, has proved important to our success so far in ridding Afghanistan of the Taliban and al-Qaida.

In Central Asia and the South Caucasus, we recognize our common interest in promoting the stability, sovereignty, and territorial integrity of all the nations of this region. The United States and Russia reject the failed model of "Great Power" rivalry that can only increase the potential for conflict in those regions. We will support economic and political development and respect for human rights while we broaden our humanitarian cooperation and cooperation on counterterrorism and counternarcotics.

The United States and Russia will cooperate to resolve regional conflicts, including those in Abkhazia and Nagorno-Karabakh, and the Transnistrian conflict in Moldova. We strongly encourage the Presidents of Azerbaijan and Armenia to exhibit flexibility and a constructive approach to resolving the conflict concerning Nagorno-Karabakh. As two of the Co-Chairmen of the OSCE's Minsk Group, the United States and Russia stand ready to assist in these efforts.

On November 13, 2001, we pledged to work together to develop a new relationship between NATO and Russia that reflects the new strategic reality in the Euro-Atlantic region. We stressed that the members of NATO and Russia are increasingly allied against terrorism, regional instability, and other contemporary threats. We therefore welcome the inauguration at the May 28, 2002, NATO-Russia summit in Rome of a new NATO-Russia Council, whose members, acting in their national capacities and in a manner consistent with their respective collective commitments and obligations, will identify common approaches, take joint decisions, and bear equal responsibility, individually and jointly, for their implementation. In this context, they will observe in good faith their obligations under international law, including the UN Charter, provisions and principles contained in the Helsinki Final Act and the OSCE Charter for European Security. In the framework of the NATO-Russia Council, NATO member states and Russia will work as equal partners in areas of common interest. They aim to stand together against common threats and risks to their security.

As co-sponsors of the Middle East peace process, the United States and Russia will continue to exert joint and parallel efforts, including in the framework of the "Quartet" to overcome the current crisis in the Middle East, to restart negotiations, and to encourage a negotiated settlement. In the Balkans, we will promote democracy, ethnic tolerance, self-sustaining peace, and long-term stability, based on respect for the sovereignty and territorial integrity of the states in the region and United Nations Security Council resolutions. The United States and Russia will continue their constructive dialogue on Iraq and welcome the continuation of special bilateral discussions that opened the way for UN Security Council adoption of the Goods Review List.

Recalling our Joint Statement of November 13, 2001, on counternarcotics cooperation, we note that illegal drug trafficking poses a threat to our peoples and to international security, and represents a substantial source of financial support for international terrorism. We are committed to intensifying cooperation against this threat, which will bolster both the security and health of the citizens of our countries.

The United States and Russia remain committed to intensifying cooperation in the fight against transnational organized crime. In this regard, we welcome the entry into force of the Treaty on Mutual Legal Assistance in Criminal Matters on January 31, 2002.

ECONOMIC COOPERATION

The United States and Russia believe that successful national development in the 21st century demands respect for the discipline and practices of the free market. As we stated on November 13, 2001, an open market economy, the freedom of economic choice, and an open democratic society are the most effective means to provide for the welfare of the citizens of our countries.

The United States and Russia will endeavor to make use of the potential of world trade to expand the economic ties between the two countries, and to further integrate Russia into the world economy as a leading participant, with full rights and responsibilities, consistent with the rule of law, in the world economic system. In this connection, the sides give high priority to Russia's accession to the World Trade Organization on standard terms.

Success in our bilateral economic and trade relations demands that we move beyond the limitations of the past. We stress the importance and desirability of graduating Russia from the emigration provisions of the US Trade Act of 1974, also known as the Jackson-Vanik Amendment. We note that the Department of Commerce, based on its ongoing thorough and deliberative inquiry, expects to make its final decision no later than June 14, 2002, on whether Russia should be treated as a market economy under the provisions of US trade law. The sides will take further practical steps to eliminate obstacles and barriers, including as appropriate in the legislative area, to strengthen economic cooperation.

We have established a new dynamic in our economic relations and between our business communities, aimed at advancing trade and investment opportunities while resolving disputes, where they occur, constructively and transparently.

The United States and Russia acknowledge the great potential for expanding bilateral trade and investment, which would bring significant benefits to both of our economies. Welcoming the recommendations of the Russian-American Business Dialogue, we are committed to working with the private sectors of our countries to realize the full potential of our economic interaction. We also welcome the opportunity to intensify cooperation in energy exploration and development, especially in oil and gas, including in the Caspian region.

STRENGTHENING PEOPLE-TO-PEOPLE CONTACTS

The greatest strength of our societies is the creative energy of our citizens. We welcome the dramatic expansion of contacts between Americans and Russians in the past ten years in many areas, including joint efforts to resolve common problems in education, health, the sciences, and environment, as well as through tourism, sister-city relationships, and other people-to-people contacts. We pledge to continue supporting these efforts, which help broaden and deepen good relations between our two countries.

Battling the scourge of HIV/AIDS and other deadly diseases, ending family violence, protecting the environment, and defending the rights of women are areas where US and Russian institutions, and especially non-governmental organizations, can successfully expand their cooperation.

PREVENTING THE SPREAD OF WEAPONS OF MASS DESTRUCTION: NON-PROLIFERATION AND INTERNATIONAL TERRORISM

The United States and Russia will intensify joint efforts to confront the new global challenges of the twenty-first century, including combating the closely linked threats of international terrorism and the proliferation of weapons of mass destruction and their means of delivery. We believe that international terrorism represents a particular danger to international stability as shown once more by the tragic events of September 11, 2001. It is imperative that all nations of the world cooperate to combat this threat decisively. Toward this end, the United States and Russia reaffirm our commitment to work together bilaterally and multilaterally.

The United States and Russia recognize the profound importance of preventing the spread of weapons of mass destruction and missiles. The specter that such weapons could fall into the hands of terrorists and those who support them illustrates the priority all nations must give to combating proliferation.

To that end, we will work closely together, including through cooperative programs, to ensure the security of weapons of mass destruction and missile technologies, information, expertise, and material. We will also continue cooperative threat reduction programs and expand efforts to reduce weapons-usable fissile material. In that regard, we will establish joint experts groups to investigate means of increasing the amount of weapons-usable fissile material to be eliminated, and to recommend collaborative research and development efforts on advanced, proliferation-resistant nuclear reactor and fuel cycle technologies. We also intend to intensify our cooperation concerning destruction of chemical weapons.

The United States and Russia will also seek broad international support for a strategy of proactive non-proliferation, including by implementing and bolstering the Treaty on the Non-Proliferation of Nuclear Weapons and the conventions on the prohibition of chemical and biological weapons. The United States and Russia call on all countries to strengthen and strictly enforce export controls, interdict illegal transfers, prosecute violators, and tighten border controls to prevent and protect against proliferation of weapons of mass destruction.

MISSILE DEFENSE, FURTHER STRATEGIC OFFENSIVE REDUCTIONS, NEW CONSULTATIVE MECHANISM ON STRATEGIC SECURITY

The United States and Russia proceed from the Joint Statements by the President of the United States of America and the President of the Russian

Federation on Strategic Issues of July 22, 2001, in Genoa and on a New Relationship Between the United States and Russia of November 13, 2001, in Washington.

The United States and Russia are taking steps to reflect, in the military field, the changed nature of the strategic relationship between them.

The United States and Russia acknowledge that today's security environment is fundamentally different than during the Cold War.

In this connection, the United States and Russia have agreed to implement a number of steps aimed at strengthening confidence and increasing transparency in the area of missile defense, including the exchange of information on missile defense programs and tests in this area, reciprocal visits to observe missile defense tests, and observation aimed at familiarization with missile defense systems. They also intend to take the steps necessary to bring a joint center for the exchange of data from early warning systems into operation.

The United States and Russia have also agreed to study possible areas for missile defense cooperation, including the expansion of joint exercises related to missile defense, and the exploration of potential programs for the joint research and development of missile defense technologies, bearing in mind the importance of the mutual protection of classified information and the safeguarding of intellectual property rights.

The United States and Russia will, within the framework of the NATO-Russia Council, explore opportunities for intensified practical cooperation on missile defense for Europe.

The United States and Russia declare their intention to carry out strategic offensive reductions to the lowest possible levels consistent with their national security requirements and alliance obligations, and reflecting the new nature of their strategic relations.

A major step in this direction is the conclusion of the Treaty Between the United States of America and the Russian Federation on Strategic Offensive Reductions.

In this connection, both sides proceed on the basis that the Treaty Between the United States of America and the Union of Soviet Socialist Republics on the Reduction and Limitation of Strategic Offensive Arms of July 31, 1991, remains in force in accordance with its terms and that its provisions will provide the foundation for providing confidence, transparency, and predictability in further strategic offensive reductions, along with other supplementary measures, including transparency measures, to be agreed.

The United States and Russia agree that a new strategic relationship between the two countries, based on the principles of mutual security, trust, openness, cooperation, and predictability requires substantive consultation across a broad range of international security issues. To that end we have decided to:

- establish a Consultative Group for Strategic Security to be chaired by Foreign Ministers and Defense Ministers with the participation of other senior officials. This group will be the principal mechanism through which the sides strengthen mutual confidence, expand transparency, share information and plans, and discuss strategic issues of mutual interest; and
- seek ways to expand and regularize contacts between our two countries' Defense Ministries and Foreign Ministries, and our intelligence agencies.

THE PRESIDENT OF THE UNITED STATES OF AMERICA
THE PRESIDENT OF THE RUSSIAN FEDERATION
Moscow
May 24, 2002.

Appendix B

*Thoughts about the Feasibility of Eliminating Nuclear Weapons**

Although some dispute the proposition that the world would be safer without nuclear weapons, most experts content themselves with saying nuclear weapons cannot be "dis-invented" and that hidden nuclear weapons could not be found. The question of whether the absence of nuclear weapons can be reliably verified is, in fact, a key issue. It obviously needs intensive study, but at least two considerations provide grounds for optimism.

First, the United States and Russia have years of successful experience in verifying numbers of operationally deployed nuclear warheads: that is, those associated with deployed missiles and bombers. Since the numbers and locations of the principal means of delivering warheads—bombers and missiles—can be monitored, this also gives us an indirect handle over non-deployed warheads. In fact, it can be argued that the task may become easier the further we progress toward zero because the rules of behavior will be well-established, which should both make anomalies easier to spot and encourage whistle blowers to speak out. Social media can be a powerful tool of verification.

Second, by the time the end state is reached, an accurate base of information about arsenals that have been built and about material that will remain subject to restraints and elimination should be in hand. During the time it will take to negotiate and implement the steps toward the end state, we can anticipate a steady accumulation of vital information. An example of this is the history of production of fissile materials, which will become better understood as time goes on. This will require extensive data exchange on past production in order to provide a baseline for judging the amount of material—HEU and Pu-239—available for nuclear bombs. With that information, the outer limits of warhead production can be predicted more accurately.

---

*Adapted from *A World Without Nuclear Weapons: End-State Issues* by Sidney Drell and James Goodby (Stanford, CA: Hoover Institution Press, 2009).

Of course, there will be difficult and complex issues with no easy answers. An example of this is the clarification of dual-use delivery vehicles, and components for space and prompt global precision conventional strike forces. But each step forward in a nuclear-restraint regime will help to build a foundation of trust, transparency, and cooperation as well as to foster improved technologies that will help meet the necessarily high standards of monitoring and verification. And lest I leave the impression that I am thinking here only of US and Russian activities, I hasten to emphasize that all nations that possess nuclear weapons would be involved in some way in a verification process. But it might not be a "one size fits all" approach. Nuclear-free zones, with appropriate verification, might be as effective as a global approach.

HOW MUCH WILL THE WORLD HAVE TO CHANGE?

Critics of the goal of eliminating nuclear weapons also say or imply that political conditions that would make elimination possible may never exist. Of course the international issues that beset us today will have to change dramatically to make possible the safe elimination of nuclear weapons. This is hardly the same as saying that world government must be achieved. It is to say that the UN Security Council will have to become a more effective instrument for ensuring compliance than it has been. There will have to be a lot of diplomacy involved—it will have to be an "Age of Diplomacy," as Secretary Shultz has called it. Nations that have acquired privileged positions in the international system by virtue of being nuclear weapons states will be reluctant to give up that status, or even to accept parity in nuclear weapons as stockpiles are reduced to low levels. Those nations that fear the conventionally armed military might of other nations will be reluctant to give up the option of a nuclear "equalizer." This is what the fatalists mean when they say the rest of the world isn't ready for such a radical idea as eliminating nuclear weapons, even if the United States is. But it is *ideas* such as these, rather than technical problems, that present the most difficult barriers to reaching zero. These are problems that can be overcome. No law of nature stands in the way.

BUILDING THE FOUNDATIONS

Even among the unconvinced, there is broad support for the more immediate steps of nuclear restraint: The Comprehensive Nuclear Test Ban Treaty; ceasing production of fissile materials for use in weapons; tightening controls over fissile materials; and internationalizing the nuclear fuel cycle. Taking these steps in the context of a serious commitment to eliminating nuclear weapons would enable the United States and other current possessors of nuclear weapons to go on the offensive in nonproliferation matters, thus enabling us to be more effective in advancing universal nonproliferation interests.

GETTING TO ZERO

Hypothetical frameworks can be developed examining key security issues that the nations will face as they approach and enter the end state. For example, there will be a need to identify conditions that would justify a final push to zero deployed and non-deployed nuclear bombs and warheads. A pause for stocktaking would be in order when nations had reduced to the level of fifty to one hundred warheads apiece, or less. The following conditions, among others, should have been met:

- Procedures for challenge inspections to search for concealed warheads had been established and satisfactorily exercised;
- Warheads scheduled for elimination could be dismantled under conditions that would assure their actual dismantling, with the nuclear components placed in secure and monitored storage pending final disposition;
- Delivery vehicles scheduled for elimination had been verifiably destroyed, and procedures were in place to confirm that dual-use systems were not armed with nuclear warheads;
- Compliance mechanisms had been established to enforce nuclear agreements;
- And beyond the nuclear aspects: advances had been made in creating and maintaining regional confidence-building and restraints regarding conventional forces; progress had been made in addressing and resolving regional disputes that threaten to trigger military actions; and international mechanisms to provide more effective compliance with nuclear agreements had been put in place.

NUCLEAR DETERRENCE AFTER ZERO

Deterrence writ large, that is, beyond the effect of nuclear weapons, relies on a variety of diplomatic, economic, and military skills and capabilities. In fact, it is arguable that these imponderables, the nonquantifiable elements of the psychological condition we call "deterrence," are more significant than the physical presence of nuclear weapons. And, in fact, nuclear deterrence will not disappear even if these weapons are eliminated. It will be manifested in a new form: the ability to reconstitute small nuclear arsenals. Jonathan Schell wrote about this in 1984, so the question "What takes the place of nuclear deterrence?" does not arise in the way the question is usually posed. For better or worse, even the power imbalances created by nuclear arsenals will not be changed that much for at least awhile after nuclear weapons have been eliminated.

In the fall of 2008, the US Secretaries of Defense and Energy issued a report in which they suggested that a "responsive nuclear infrastructure" would make it possible, over time, for the United States to rely less on non-deployed nuclear warheads. This should also permit a lower level of deployed warheads. A responsive nuclear infrastructure means functioning nuclear laboratories and some capacity to produce nuclear weapons, if needed, in a timely way. This may be what nuclear deterrence will look like in the future. For the purists, it is not ideal. But it is a big improvement over what we have today.

This type of deterrence would not only serve as a deterrent against other nations' use of a concealed nuclear weapon and their reconstitution of small nuclear arsenals. It should also preserve the risk that engaging in a major war fought with conventional weapons would most likely lead to nuclear conflict.

CONTROLLING RECONSTITUTION

During the final approach to zero, those nations possessing nuclear weapons almost certainly will maintain a basic nuclear infrastructure sufficient to ensure the effectiveness of their shrinking stockpile, including a hedge capability to reconstitute nuclear forces if necessary. This capability for reconstitution will not automatically disappear once all nuclear weapons have been eliminated. Of course this poses a daunting challenge to the whole idea of going to zero. Would it be an invitation to a reconstitution race? Could conditions of stable deterrence be developed under such conditions? Does getting to zero offer realistic prospects for establishing a *safer* world—not a safe one—but *safer* than less radical alternatives for reducing nuclear arms and limiting their spread? To minimize this risk of breakout instability, agreement on three key questions will be necessary:

1. What are the necessary elements of an adequate nuclear infrastructure, that is, one with a capacity for limited and timely reconstitution of a deterrent?
2. What activities, facilities, or weapons-related items should be limited or prohibited?

3. What can be done to assure early and reliable warning of a breakout attempt?

All this illustrates, as emphasized more than two decades ago by Jonathan Schell and later by Michael Mazarr, nuclear deterrence based on virtual nuclear arsenals will exist even after reaching zero. We will have banned the existence of a ready-to-use arsenal, but not eliminated the capability to build one—perhaps even rapidly—if absolutely necessary. But I think it is worth emphasizing that inevitably, as confidence increases in managing stability in a world without nuclear weapons, disparities in nuclear capabilities will decrease over time between those states that possessed nuclear weapons and those that had not done so. It will be a major challenge to monitor and verify permissible activities that are part of a responsive nuclear infrastructure, even after reaching zero, until such a capability withers away.

Appendix C

Draft Agreement on the Nuclear Test Moratorium

by
THOMAS GRAHAM*

The States Signatory to this Agreement, either now or later, hereinafter referred to as "The Parties,"

Aware that the five nuclear weapon states recognized by the Treaty on the Non-Proliferation of Nuclear Weapons have adopted voluntary nuclear test moratoria and have observed these moratoria for nearly twenty years, that several other states with nuclear weapon programs outside of the treaty regime have also been observing moratoria for many years and that only one state—in recent years—has taken action contrary to this widely recognized and now long lasting norm of international practice,

Noting the objective expressed by the Parties to the 1963 Treaty Banning Nuclear Weapon Tests in the Atmosphere, in Outer Space and Under Water to seek to achieve the discontinuance of all test explosions of nuclear weapons for all time and to continue negotiations to that end,

Recognizing the reaffirmation of this objective in the Preamble to the Treaty on the Non-Proliferation of Nuclear Weapons,

Emphasizing that the cessation of all nuclear weapon test explosions will contribute to the non-proliferation of nuclear weapons in all its aspects, to the process of nuclear disarmament leading toward complete elimination of nuclear weapons and, therefore, to the further enhancement of peace and security,

Convinced that the most effective way to achieve an end to nuclear testing is by means of the entry into force of the universal and effectively verifiable Comprehensive Test Ban Treaty signed in 1996, which has long

---

*Thomas Graham is the former general counsel of the US Arms Control and Disarmament Agency. Reproduced with permisson.

been one of the highest priority objectives of the international community in the field of disarmament and non-proliferation,

Supporting the continuance of the Moratorium on nuclear weapon test explosions pending the entry into force of the Comprehensive Test Ban Treaty,

Recognizing the importance of expanding the adherents to the Moratorium to all states and to that end, recording certain mutual understandings regarding the Moratorium,

Have agreed as follows:

1. A nuclear explosion for the purpose of monitoring compliance with the Moratorium shall be considered to be any explosion resulting from a self-sustaining nuclear chain reaction.
2. The Parties to this Agreement shall provide each other information from time to time to strengthen confidence in the Moratorium.
3. Any State Party that is a recognized nuclear weapon state under the Treaty on the Non-Proliferation of Nuclear Weapons or is a state in possession of nuclear weapons outside the Treaty as of the date of this Agreement on a reciprocal basis as it deems appropriate, may invite any other such Party to visit its declared nuclear weapon test site.
4. Any State Party of the type covered by Paragraph 3 may, as it deems appropriate, agree to employ agreed sensors at test sites to provide monitoring capabilities to other such State Parties, on a reciprocal basis. As appropriate, this information may be shared with the International Monitoring System in the Comprehensive Test Ban Treaty Office.
5. The States Parties of the type covered in Paragraph 3, may, on a reciprocal basis, share information on the subject of maintaining the integrity of their nuclear weapons with other States Parties covered by Paragraph 3.
6. States Parties shall consult with one another concerning the nuclear weapon test activities of other states.
7. The States Parties invite other states, whether or not members of the Treaty on the Non-Proliferation of Nuclear Weapons, to join them as parties to this Agreement.
8. This Agreement shall remain in force until the entry into force of the Comprehensive Test Ban Treaty. Any State Party may withdraw from this Agreement upon three months' notice.

In witness whereof, the undersigned, duly authorized, have signed this Agreement.

INDEX

About the Author

James E. Goodby. As a member of the U.S. Foreign Service, he achieved the rank of Career Minister, was appointed ambassador to Finland, and held three other ambassadorial-level assignments. He has taught at Georgetown, Syracuse, and Carnegie Mellon Universities. Ambassador Goodby is an Annenberg Distinguished Visiting Fellow at the Hoover Institution. During his foreign service career, he was involved as a negotiator or as a policy adviser in the creation of the International Atomic Energy Agency, the negotiation of the limited nuclear test ban treaty, NATO's preparations for the Conference on Security and Co-operation in Europe, START, the Conference on Disarmament in Europe, and cooperative threat reduction (the Nunn-Lugar program). Goodby is the author and editor of several books. His most recent publication is *The War That Must Never Be Fought: Dilemmas of Nuclear Deterrence* (Hoover Institution Press, 2015) edited with George P. Shultz. Among his other publications are *At the Borderline of Armageddon: How American Presidents Managed the Atom Bomb* (Rowman & Littlefield Publishers, 2006) and *Europe Undivided: The New Logic of Peace in US-Russian Relations* (Washington, DC: United States Institute of Peace Press, 1998). He is the first winner of the Heinz Award in Public Policy and holds the Commander's Cross, Order of Merit of Germany.

See more at:
http://www.hoover.org/profiles/james-goodby
https://www.wilsoncenter.org/person/ambassador-james-goodby#
sthash.uGCcjK7C.dpuf

www.ingramcontent.com/pod-product-compliance
Lightning Source LLC
Chambersburg PA
CBHW022320280326
41932CB00010B/1171